GARY COOPER

David Thomson is, among many other things, the author of *The New Biographical Dictionary of Film*, now in its fourth edition. His recent books include a biography of Nicole Kidman, completing and editing *Fan Tan* (a novel started by Marlon Brando and Donald Cammell), and *The Whole Equation: A History of Hollywood*. His latest work is the acclaimed *Have You Seen . . . ? A Personal Introduction to 1,000 Films*. Born in London, he now lives in San Francisco.

Books in the GREAT STARS Series
by David Thomson

Ingrid Bergman
Humphrey Bogart
Gary Cooper
Bette Davis

GARY COOPER

GARY COOPER

David Thomson

PHOTO RESEARCH BY LUCY GRAY

ff Faber and Faber, Inc.

An affiliate of Farrar, Straus and Giroux

New York

GREAT STARS

Faber and Faber, Inc.
An affiliate of Farrar, Straus and Giroux
18 West 18th Street, New York 10011

Copyright © 2009 by David Thomson
All rights reserved
Printed in the United States of America
Originally published in 2009 by Penguin Books, Great Britain
Published in the United States by Faber and Faber, Inc.
First American edition, 2010

Library of Congress Cataloging-in-Publication Data
Thomson, David, 1941–
    Gary Cooper / David Thomson ; photo research by Lucy Gray. —
1st American ed.
        p.   cm.— (Great stars)
    ISBN: 978-0-86547-932-6 (pbk. : alk. paper)
    1. Cooper, Gary, 1901–1961.   2. Motion picture actors and actresses—
United States—Biography.   I. Title.

PN2287.C59T46 2010
791.4302'8092—dc22
[B]

                                                                    2009041759

www.fsgbooks.com

1   3   5   7   9   10   8   6   4   2

For Joseph

GARY COOPER

Gary Cooper died six days after his sixtieth birthday, on 13 May 1961, having made over a hundred movies. Only a couple of weeks before his own death – when that outcome was certain – he and his wife, Rocky, sent a cable to their friend Ernest Hemingway. They had heard that the depressed author was having electroshock treatment. All they said in the cable was, 'What's there to say except that you have our love?' They were not close enough to Hemingway to know all his troubles, from paranoia to writer's block to impotence and the impenetrable gloom he called the black dog days. Hemingway shot himself that 2 July, early in the morning, while his wife was still asleep. He rested his forehead against the shotgun barrels and tripped the triggers. Cooper and Hemingway had a regard for each other – they had mutual respect and they reckoned that the other man was part of their meaning. And they were gone in the same season.

And in 1961, of course, John F. Kennedy was busy with his efforts to be president. On 17 April, with unofficial US support, some Cuban exiles invaded Cuba at the Bahía de Cochinos. At the time, it seemed like a shaming debacle – years later it is not much less than a day of infamy. Hemingway still had a house in Cuba, as well as many friends there. Gary Cooper was of the right wing politically, so it's hard to say what he thought of the Bay of Pigs – if he was able to take it in. Perhaps he was sheltered by his wife in the last days just as Mary Welsh did what she could to protect Hemingway. She even announced that his death was accidental, one of those mistakes men make with guns. As if Papa could endure a headline with 'gun accident' in it – it was like writing an accidental masterpiece. Still, it was a bad season for American heroes such as Hemingway, Cooper and Kennedy. But worse was to come.

I am reminded of an extraordinarily beautiful photograph. It's taken some time around 1942, with two men at a restaurant or a bar table, both of them leaning back to get a proper look at the other. They are Gary Cooper and Jack Kennedy: the one is a lieutenant in navy uniform, and the other may be making *Ball of Fire* or even *For Whom the Bell Tolls*. Kennedy is younger by far, and he is with a movie star and one he admires. You can feel that warmth and affection in Jack's grin. But Coop knows who Jack is, too. He's Hollywood enough to know the Kennedy story and to know how much support there is already for the lieutenant. He also admires and may be a touch daunted by the boy's Pacific suntan and the idea that this kid goes to sea on not much more than a platform with a gun and makes faces at the Japanese. Not to mention the purchasing power at legend's store that the Kennedy family had available.

They like each other and they seem amused by the

notion that they represent different strands of heroism, the real thing and the movie version. Yet they're close enough in age to be likely rivals for some young woman who isn't in the picture yet. She's powdering her nose wondering who takes her back to the hotel. They both fancy their chances, while esteeming the competitor. Their self-confidence is a great part of what makes them attractive. So they haven't the faintest idea that the spring of 1961 is going to be a pretty rough time for them – they haven't read those papers yet.

They are two beautiful guys, and in 1942 there was still no doubt about Cooper's handsomeness or his casual eminence. He might not be exactly the laconic angel he had been in 1930 or so, when every photographer in town wanted to shoot him. But Coop was still untroubled, despite a face which, as he said, had lines from being out-of-doors so much by the time he was twenty. Yet there are troubled moments in *Mr. Deeds Goes to Town* (1936), brief passages where the good-natured Cooper seems to conceive of something ugly, something grave, something as awful as his own failure.

One of the openings available for a book like this is the chance to detect when it is that anxiety creeps into Coop's looks. Certainly it is there by the time of *High Noon* (1952), but you could say that it's there because it needs to be – because Sheriff Will Kane faces a kind of social betrayal, not to mention death, in his own town. But *High Noon* comes soon after *The Fountainhead* (1949), a very important Cooper film, and the occasion of the

Twentieth-century cowboy

greatest threat and disruption in his real life. That is when he nearly went off with another woman, Patricia Neal.

Of course, you can look further ahead, to the haggard, nearly agonized faces he offered the fifties in *Love in the Afternoon*, *Ten North Frederick*, *Man of the West* or *They Came to Cordura* where he sometimes seems much older or far more stricken than a man in his fifties. But perhaps he was ill aready then, struggling to hold on, or aware that his pure heroism was not quite enough to let a man go all the way. Gary Cooper was not really ambitious. In all those films, he never wrote or directed. Only on one occasion did he try to produce – and that fun wore off fast. He did what was offered, without pursuing projects or parts. He had no great opinion of himself as an actor, and so he did not seem to seek out large and challenging parts. He never really took on the novelty of playing an older man in a young person's world. He was always the lead, with action scenes, ever younger actresses opposite him, and with the weight of the film on his face. But something happened, and in any retrospective of Gary Cooper's films you cannot miss the sense of osteoporosis or nervousness that eventually overtakes a great American tree.

It's a matter of fact that director Fred Zinnemann had thought of either Marlon Brando or Montgomery Clift for Sheriff Kane in *High Noon*. Those two actors were twenty years younger than Cooper, which made it more plausible that Kane has just married Grace Kelly

(twenty-four to Cooper's fifty-one in 1952). That gap is
never addressed, but it surely adds to our sense of Kane as
a man left stranded by his world. Cooper's anguish is that
of someone beginning to feel his age and the strange dis-
pensation of a late but true marriage. *High Noon* would
work with Clift – no doubt about that – but Kane would
feel like a more ordinary guy. In Cooper's stooped, fragile
form he becomes a relic of a lost West. Part of his distress
is in realizing how far standards have broken down. And
when he sees his wife riding to the railroad depot, it is as if
all of his life is ebbing already. In the young wife, we can
feel his hope and his hopelessness. Of course, in real life,
things were not as subtle: like opportunists, careless of the
large separation in their roles, Cooper and Kelly just had an
affair on location.

Frank James Cooper was born 7 May 1901 in a good
house, with railings around its yard, in Helena, Montana. He was the second child of two emigrants from
England, and although he grew up as a young cowboy,
he was also raised in a tradition of English order and
gentility. So he was one of the relatively few movie cowboys born to the job, but he was a tall beauty who also
learned to appreciate the best clothes. He was torn over
the two ways to go, and a story was told how once upon
a time – as a young movie star – he had been invited out
by one of those ladies he dazzled, the Countess Dorothy di Frasso. So he got the best tuxedo he could find, a
silk top hat, the finest English shoes and a chic cloak.

There he was, waiting for the Countess's car. A fashion plate. And the chauffeur drew up beside him and murmured, 'Get in, cowboy.'

Frank's father, Charles, was born in Dunstable, Bedfordshire, England, in 1865, to a well-to-do farming family. But by the time he was twenty he was living in Montana and beginning to study law. The population of the state was no more than a hundred thousand, but it mined a quarter of the world's copper. It was in mining towns – like Helena and Butte – that the state was crowded, and where championship fights might be held to attract the miners as well as the cowboys and ranchers. And as he developed as a lawyer, Charles Cooper met Alice Louise Brazier. She was of Huguenot descent from a family of shopkeepers on the north Kent coast. Born in Sheerness in 1873, she was in Montana by the time she was eighteen. They were a natural couple, not just because they had chosen to set out for the New World and its beautiful open spaces, but because in doing so they had left a part of themselves and their security behind. They missed England, and Englishness, and so their son Frank grew up accustomed to the wild life of an actor in Westerns but unable to resist the pull of an older, more controlled society, where manners made the man, and the practice of law might tame human vagary.

So Gary Cooper rode with uncommon ease, which means that his horse, his hat and a gun were ways of revealing himself – as natural as gesture or sunlight. At

the same time, the father whom Cooper adored was a
law-and-order man who ended up on the state supreme
court and who knew when to go after the big copper
companies and the railroads – an independent man
whose sense of the law might stand behind a small-
town sheriff like Will Kane.

More or less, we owe the existence of Gary Cooper
to the way in which two politely raised young English
people ventured six thousand miles away from home
and found each other in a wilderness where civilized society had a still uncertain foothold. As lately as 1876 –
in the Montana Territory – Custer and the 7th Cavalry
had been wiped out by a great army of Sioux and Chey-
enne. Not that the Indians could ever hold what they
had won or survive rebuke. But the event of the Little
Bighorn had exposed for anyone to see the way in
which sheer outlawry could take over the law and
rewrite it as it wished. The new white Americans were
determined to take the rich land, and they came close to
expunging the red race that owned it first. In that situation, the law was a very practical instrument, with
bloody hands and a wounded conscience. Violence was
heavy in the unpoliced air. It was as Cooper's parents
arrived in America that the Johnson County War was
being fought in Wyoming – not too far away – in a desperate struggle between vested landowners and the
immigrant rabble (this is the story of *Heaven's Gate*).

So, in all the talk of heaven and the easy idealization
of a young Frank Cooper as the model for Remington

paintings of the cowboy at liberty, never forget the real pressures of the new land. By 1952, Will Kane is good and his opponents are unequivocally wicked. But then consider how far the *High Noon* set piece may have been little more than the confrontation of rival gangsters and power-dealers such as occurred at the OK Corral in Tombstone in 1881. The openness of the West was an opportunity for making the laws that suited you, so the law quickly became a pressure for conservative reform – because you weren't going to get new settlers in the West so long as they thought it was too dangerous for their wives and children.

So it's legitimate and accurate to see Frank Cooper as a kid on horseback as naturally as Huck Finn telling a story. Frank knew ranchers and trail-drivers, miners and their whores. Not to mention Indians. He was very likely smoking cigarettes. There was no way of fencing off the proximity of such sights. But he had parents who noticed these developing traits, who heard his frontier language, and who decided that he must be sent back to Dunstable to be tamed. It's as if the parents had not yet decided fully on being American, or on accepting that hell to which Huck consigns himself.

And so, in the summer of 1909, Frank and his brother, Arthur (five years older), were taken to England by their mother, and installed with uncles and aunts so that they could attend Dunstable School. They stayed there until the spring of 1913.

Cooper never complained about Dunstable School,

no matter that he was cut off from his parents, mocked first for his American accent and then later for his English intonation. In later life, he revisited the school several times and gave every sign of fondness for his English cousins and his Edwardian upbringing. He learned French and some Latin; he could recite English poetry; and he was a loyal member of a generation that was destined for Flanders. Cooper's best biographer, Jeffrey Meyers, notes that sixty-two graduates from Dunstable School would lose their lives in the First World War.

It was a moment of uncritical patriotism and team spirit in which the schools were a vital part of the effort to build morale and discipline at the same time. Thus, Cooper was in England – and earnest to do his best – in almost exactly the time period of Captain Robert Scott's fatal expedition to the South Pole. In what turned into a race with the Norwegians, led by Roald Amundsen, Scott's party despaired of motor sledges, ponies and dogs and ended up man-hauling their geological specimens and the tent they used against the blizzard. The last five of them died in what was either immense British heroism and dedication, or misguided planning. Frank Cooper would have had no doubt about the British valour. Cooper never served in the armed forces, but just consider the list of films in which he is a follower of the code or the regiment (sometimes tested, but always loyal) – *Wings*; *Morocco*; *Today We Live*; *The Lives of a Bengal Lancer*; *Beau Geste*; *North West Mounted*

Police; *Sergeant York*; *The Pride of the Yankees*; *For Whom the Bell Tolls*; *Unconquered*; *Task Force*; *High Noon*; *Springfield Rifle*; *The Court Martial of Billy Mitchell*; *Man of the West*; *They Came to Cordura*.

You might argue that every male star in the years 1930–60 could boast as many films hinged on loyalty and service. And there's something in that – the code was a cover-all. But then notice how many other male stars handled duty through degrees of rebellion or disenchantment – Cagney, Bogart, Cary Grant – and you begin to see Cooper's unique openness to the unwritten or unspoken code. You can make fun of it – 'A man's got to do what a man's got to do' – but I don't think Cooper ever felt the irony or the risk of cliché. He may not have been the brightest movie star we ever had. He may have elected to be more a doer than someone who reflected over decisions. But he could make the effort of arriving at an honourable decision seem fresh every time.

It reminds me of a story told by Niven Busch, who was for a time a story editor at the Goldwyn company where Cooper was under contract. The two men were friends; they had shared sporting tastes. And sometimes Coop would drop in on Busch as the Princeton graduate wrestled with a story outline. When Busch admitted he couldn't solve it, Cooper said, 'Well, Niven, seems to me if you make me the hero it usually comes out right.'

Busch chuckled. He thought the actor was telling a

joke, or making fun of an excessive personal vanity. But then he looked at Cooper's level gaze and realized that, no, the actor had only just worked it out and was trying to be helpful: 'Make me the hero and it usually comes out right.' It was as if Cooper had no hint of the way nature and the camera had made that pact so long ago – and that it was a curiosity that no one ever asked him to play a bad guy. Yet a man subject to weakness or temptation – that was another matter. Women said that if only Gary Cooper hadn't been so shy, the army of those he seduced might have been smaller.

Cooper would say later that he was irked by some English things – small, overly tidy gardens, the Eton collars he had to wear, and the damp weather. But observers at the time felt he was happy enough. He grew much closer to his older brother, and did not make too much of missing his parents. He dressed like a Montana hooligan, maybe, but along the way he picked up a taste for English tailoring and very good clothes. He was tall and more than good-looking, and if the two things weren't always the same, still, he was interested in being good and looking good. But if put to the test, he was more for looking good.

He came back to Montana as if he had never been away. He was riding again and taking his sketchbook into deep country. His drawings were skilful if not very personal, but they showed his rapport with nature. By now his father had a small ranch, so the open-air life came naturally. There would be a summer when Frank took a job as a guide for tourist parties at Yellowstone National Park. When Arthur enlisted in the army, in 1917, Frank worked on the family ranch, growing alfalfa and herding cattle. At the age of sixteen, it was said, he grew an inch a month for over a year and soon he was six foot three, with dark blonde hair and the kind of composed inward glance that already seemed to tease the camera.

But in 1917, he was injured in an automobile accident where the car rolled over several times. At this distance, it's not quite clear what happened, but some accounts suggest Frank suffered and endured a broken hip that was left to heal naturally. Can such things happen? He said he had to learn to ride again, and he would claim that it left his walk a little unbalanced. Who knows? There are times when Cooper seems to walk with uncommon grace – yet at others, it is a cautious walk. It may have been an exaggerated affair around which Frank built his own legend of being tentative. In later life, he was known as a very good skier and a natural horseman. But when Will Kane walks down the deserted street you can see that a tall man does take rather mincing steps, as if afraid that he might snap or collapse. These are some of the ways a movie actor conjures with his own self. You see, often enough Gary Cooper said nothing or very little, but he could not avoid moving across the frame. He walked – and he had given himself away. Observers reported that Cooper was often indifferent to his lines, but that he would rehearse small gestures until they were engraved. So he understood his medium.

The story is still told how visitors to a Gary Cooper set could not understand what was going on. They watched. They peered. They saw nothing happening in a scene where Coop had drained away what little he had had to say. (He was always inclined to cut or foreshorten his own lines.) 'Remarkable!' pronounced the visitors. 'Perhaps it is a bad day for him.' But then the next day they saw the dailies and Cooper held the screen – his waiting face, his coiled body – there was nothing else to see. The magic had worked. But very often in those stories, it was simply that he was saying nothing. He was watching the process of film-making and using his great will to rest – just as if it was the coming of the four outlaws in *High Noon*. It was not that Coop was unafraid. But in silence and waiting he could let that fear hide, so that as you watched you hardly knew if he was afraid or very dangerous. Sometimes it is enough to deliver that quality of apprehension or patience in just a couple of shots. And more than other stars in this series, Gary Cooper seems to have known that his secret and his being had little to do with the sustained workings of script or story – they were there in just a couple of shots, so long as his character had been given the shine of virtue when virtue was a close call.

Apart from drawing well, he showed no special aptitude at high school. His graduation was a bit of a scramble with a few courses picked up at the Montana Agricultural College. He did some newspaper work; he sold advertising space door to door. He went away to Iowa to attend Grinnell College and he appeared in a play there – he seemed to like it, though in matters of vocation it was said that the consumption of pancakes was more in his line. There is a style of American acting – tight-lipped and laconic – that does seem to be imagining a feast, while regarding it as a fool's dream. This is a point fit for adding, that Gary Cooper reportedly ate like a horse at every opportunity and hardly ever put on any flesh.

There was no question of the law being his destiny, and so when his father retired from the Montana Supreme Court, the parents decided to move to Los Angeles. At least they didn't go back to Dunstable – and this may have been because Frank's mother already showed every sign of being determined to look after a boy who didn't have enough concern for his own future. In which case, the move to Los Angeles was inspired. It wasn't long after Frank Cooper hit town – in 1925 – that he bumped into some chums from Montana, notably Jay Talbott, sometimes known as 'Slim'. Talbott was already employed on routine Western movies – serials very often – as a rider and a supplier of horses. These two trades went together, and required the rough-and-tumble skill of being able to ride a falling horse and then shoot the horse if it was too seriously injured. He told Frank it was easy enough money, and Frank seemed to agree that it was better than work. Jay Talbott would serve as Cooper's stunt-rider for the entirety of his career.

If it seems like a half-hearted career decision, remember that in no more than five years Gary Cooper was a movie star earning a fortune. He took some advice: he changed his name from 'Frank' to 'Gary'. He paid for a personal screen test. And – of course – he took it for granted that movies would abide by their present, rather staid condition – they would stay silent. If he'd known he'd have to talk, he might have remained in Montana.

He had made several tiny appearances as an extra before he found himself taken off to a far location, the Black Rock desert, in Nevada, for *The Winning of Barbara Worth* (1926). It was a Ronald Colman picture, directed by Henry King, a tale of dams and floods. There was a character, 'Abe Lee', who has to make an immense ride carrying news of a flood. The original actor for the role wasn't on location on the right day, so Cooper got the part instead. He was noticed, it was said, because someone saw the way he blew dust from the surface of water before taking a drink. It was a touch of authenticity in a very contrived movie. The director took Coop aside and impressed upon him the length of the ride and the state of exhaustion. He was to come up to the door and fall flat on his face. 'Don't break your fall,' said Henry King. 'You're too tired.'

'Got it,' said Cooper. He looked haggard and half-buried from dust. And when he got to the door he fell

like a tree – only the skill of Ronald Colman prevented
him from hurting himself. There was applause. The kid
had pulled it off – just one moment of extremism, and
a willingness to be committed for it. He had to die, too,
of course, so 'I just lay in Colman's arms and pretended
I was taking a nap.' Everyone who saw the picture
remembered the moment – including Clara Bow, who
had a lap ready for any good-looking guy tempted to
fall.

Clara Bow was four years younger than Gary Cooper
but a couple of years ahead of him in the picture business. She was a sexpot of the moment, but one whose
popularity owed everything to her vivacity and her
bursting good humour. Nobody has ever had quite as
much fun being sexy on screen, or has indicated that
the real thing was far better. Bow came from impover-
ished roots in Brooklyn and she had had an unstable
mother. But for a few years she was a self-bottled cham-
pagne as well as a young woman who believed in having
a good time. She was called the 'It' girl because she
starred in the movie of that name taken from the Eli-
nor Glyn novel about a racy modern woman. And
Bow's pull was sufficient then for this pine-tree cowboy,
Gary Cooper, to have a small part in *It*, and to be the
open squire to the happy-go-lucky star.

It all ended badly. Sound and puritanical reactions
eroded Clara Bow's brief fame. She had breakdowns
and she suffered the legend of her own promiscuity.
But for a year or two that legend was simply living fact,

and Bow and Cooper were a couple who enjoyed each other enormously, without shame or discretion. Indeed, it was the delighted Bow – she had wide, surprised eyes like Marilyn Monroe's – who let it be known that Gary Cooper was an exceptionally well-endowed lover, and insatiable yet very tender to the ladies. What can the historian say? It's very clear that many women were thrilled to have sex with Cooper and that can only have been aided if he was better hung than most of the competition. Of course, there is also a strange natural affinity between his sustained pauses and the ladies' sighs of rapture. We are tempted to believe in it. But measurements do not survive – a lesson to every aspiring 'cocksman', and a gentle reminder to make the best of what you've got while you can. Inches are not everything, they say. Still, a few extra where you didn't expect to find them is at least a bonus.

Bow's stardom rubbed off on Coop, just as his prowess grew in the telling. In *It*, he has one scene – that of a reporter taking notes. He's gone in an instant but you remember him, and you feel the unquestioned wash of Bow's generosity. If nothing else, she taught the handsome guy that you got paid for being in pictures in several different ways. This was a habit that he would never drop – along with shortening every line of dialogue whenever he could. By the time Cooper was secure, Bow was out of pictures. Yet if you look at her work today, you are easily carried back to her riotous affair with the public. She is a sensation, and there must have been heady days and nights as she and Coop had their couple of years together. She taught him that pictures ought to be easy, or natural.

Bow is the female lead in *Wings*, of course – though not the most plausible First World War nurse on the books. But as that enormous production went on location, so Coop came along, too, as Bow's room-mate – their arrangement seems to have been flagrantly open and in the spirit of recklessness to be found at the time. The stars of the film were Buddy Rogers and Richard Arlen, and they quickly co-opted Coop as one of their gang. But again, he has just one small scene in *Wings* – that of a veteran pilot who salutes the two rookies and goes off to his own death. There is the same force as there was in *It* and *The Winning of Barbara Worth*. You wonder for a moment why Coop isn't doing the Arlen part, but then you realize that his fatalism, his knowledge, is already too dark for those boys. But the point is left very clearly: sooner or later someone is going to make a whole movie around this Gary Cooper, his beauty and the sardonic, shy grin. What was in view, as never before, was something we might call underacting – it was as if Gary Cooper had an intuition that sound was coming to the aid of the raw young medium. And once the pictures could talk then a guy could stay quiet without having to signal that decision in gaudy pantomime. He could do nothing except wait like a gunfighter at high noon.

Not talking was a measure of manliness. Sooner or

later, talk led to doubt and confusion, to explaining yourself, whereas the icon that Cooper presented – gaunt,
lean, watchful and poised – was a sufficient signal system. Such men did not tell women they loved them; they
did not need to warn other men to keep off their territory. They simply indicated the threat of male violence,
and there is no question that as the movies took on
sound so they accommodated violence – there was the
smack of blows and the snap of gunfire; there was
the disturbance of a great fight scene (such as Coop
had in *The Spoilers*, 1930). But the silence of a man spoken to was potentially violent, too. In *The Virginian*
(1929), Owen Wister's classic Western novel and a key
picture for the actor, Cooper's hero tells another man,
'If you want to call me that – smile when you say it.'
(Thirty years later, in a London restaurant, Charlton
Heston saw and heard Coop use the same line to silence
some rowdies.) The lines rapidly became clichés, of
course, and an extra part of the manly code came into
being – that the lines could often be cut and replaced
with a look. Cooper carried this non-committal attitude
to its limit, but only because of his bleak confidence
and the concomitant realization that he was scooping
up most of the girls attached to a picture.

Lupe Velez wasn't in *The Virginian* – its heroine was
the demure Mary Brian – but Velez was another of the
women who found Coop irresistible, and so she took
off on location with the unit, no matter that she had
already had an affair with the film's director, Victor

Lupe and Coop

Fleming. Maria Guadalupe Velez de Villalobos was only in her early twenties, but she was 'the Mexican spitfire' in every man's imagination. She was funny, animated and fair value as an actress – but much better and more uninhibited in person. And just like Clara Bow, she couldn't stop talking about Coop and his primordial equipment. No such thing exists, of course, but there could surely have been a great scene where an actor like Cooper did a very slow, taciturn burn while a woman like Velez gabbled away in her account of his manhood. He was fifteen inches taller than she was, but it was the old story about inches having their place and their legend.

In all of this, Cooper's mother Alice was a steadfast cheerleader. It wasn't clear that anything needed to be said about what was going on between Coop and Lupe, but when her boy played with Evelyn Brent in *Beau Sabreur* (1928), Alice Cooper volunteered for anyone interested: 'Evelyn Brent has been good for Gary; she has given him poise, she has taught him to think, her influence has been excellent, and I will always regard her with affection and gratitude.' (It's a pity that we don't have Mrs Cooper's informed rating of the entire field with which her son ran.)

And by far the most important and educational exchange occurred with Marlene Dietrich in *Morocco* (1930) – in many senses it may have been the most influential film Coop ever made. The director, Josef von Sternberg, had just gone to Berlin to make *Der blaue Engel – The Blue Angel*, a film in both German and English, the story of the humiliation of a pompous school-teacher, Professor Rath (Emil Jannings), by a cabaret singer, Lola-Lola (Dietrich). Sternberg claimed that he had gone to Berlin just to work with the great Jannings again on an artistic film – they had done *The Last Command* together in Hollywood. Perhaps. On screen, it looks like a journey with assassination in mind. And once in Berlin, Sternberg made it clear that while he took Rath for granted, he was obsessed with the need to find someone new and dangerous as Lola-Lola. Many young women were considered, but the choice fell on Dietrich, at that time a nearly plump, but sly, singer who had made a few pictures without leaving much of an impression.

The Blue Angel changed everything, though UFA, the German studio, could not quite appreciate Dietrich at first. That's how Sternberg won her for Paramount and ensured that she would be coming to America as his great star and his personal mistress. As they said farewell in Berlin – they were both married to others – she is said to have given him a book, *Amy Jolly: Woman of Marrakesh*, by Benno Vigny, as material for their first American film. Sternberg would rename it *Morocco*.

This is the stuff of movie legend, with Sternberg and Dietrich making six films at Paramount that are a bittersweet portrait of their tenuous romance, and one of the screen's most complete tributes to passionate love standing above all else. There's no need to argue that *Morocco* is the best of the six, but every reason to point

out that the male figures in many of the series are
ciphers and gestures in the empire that is Marlene. But
Legionnaire Tom Brown – Cooper's role in *Morocco* –
may be the most challenging male in the six films. That's
reason enough to suppose that when he and she looked
upon each other there was no resisting the total inevita-
bility of a love affair. More to the point, Cooper holds
his own against her in the film. The establishment at
Paramount acclaimed the actress (with good reason),
but the film was a major step in Cooper's progress.

What can we say about Tom Brown, except that we
know nothing about him except for the way Cooper's
long body lolls in a chair and the profound mixture of
respect, lust and poker-faced amusement with which
he regards the phenomenon of Amy Jolly. The film is
made around her. Sternberg might have felt once that
nearly any decent-looking actor would suffice to gaze at
her. But Cooper's lazy alertness, his wicked sultriness
and his plain awe of Amy take the film much further
than that. At first, Sternberg had wanted John Gilbert
(the most romantic actor of the silent era), and then his
thoughts turned to Fredric March. But he agreed to use
Cooper, no matter that Sternberg had passed on trying
to improve *Children of Divorce* (a Cooper–Clara Bow picture) on the grounds that it was a forlorn venture.

We have no notion of why Tom Brown is in the Foreign Legion. We know he is American – that is all – plus
the fact that he manages to make the legionnaire's uniform seem like one of the ideal fashion statements of

With Dietrich in *Morocco*

the '30s. Cooper was heroic, of course, in his own mind as much as in his scripts. He was manly, tall, ruggedly handsome. He was a man for a fight. But so many films cannot help but disclose moments when he has an elegance not far short of Fred Astaire. In wearing clothes, in looking at someone, in pausing before a movement, he personifies grace without ever hinting at the brittleness that was never too far away with John Gilbert. The first time we see Brown, in the cabaret, the way he moves across the scene to find a seat is a model of this fluency. It could easily be missed – yet it is close kin to the delicious hesitations in everything Dietrich does. And throughout *Morocco*, we have the feeling of two very self-sufficient icons going to school on each other. The touchstone to this mutuality is the little mockery of a salute – military, yet intimate, too – with which both characters greet each other.

The story is very simple, very blunt – it can easily be misunderstood. Amy Jolly comes to Morocco, as an entertainer. In the first third of the film we see her on shipboard – mysterious, cryptic but solitary – and then in her great act, the one where she wears a tuxedo, takes a flower from a young woman's hair (the bloom is soon given to Brown) and, after a languid pause, kisses her. A woman in pants. A woman prepared to acknowledge lesbian charm. And yet a standard version of the screen's orthodoxy – that the entertainer is metaphor for a whore.

Men want Amy – above all, LaBessiere (Adolphe Menjou), polite, whippable (we anticipate his own

defeat), and surely intended to resemble Sternberg. Tom
Brown sees into Amy, adores her and acknowledges rapport. Yet he will not be cosy, comfortable or com-
promised with her. She cannot resist that fond distance
he keeps. And so, finally, as he sets off into the desert
(filmed at Guadalupe in California), she abandons civilized life and joins the gang of Arab camp followers that
pursue the Legion. There is a huge spade-shaped arch
through which we see the desert and the retreating column. In a fashionable dress, a Hermès scarf and high-
heeled shoes, Amy follows him – it is abasement, but it
is levitation, too, just as it is one of the great moments
of camp ecstasy in American film, a drastic sundering of
censorship and politeness, as raw as the fucking that
cannot be shown or alluded to.

You can argue that *Morocco* is an American con-
venience, in that the man is left supreme or impreg-
nable, not even humbled by the admission of love that
is central in *Shanghai Express*. So *Morocco* may seem to
celebrate Dietrich's perverse ungraspability while turning her into a kind of slave. But that is the outline of the
action, not the feeling of the film. Attended to on screen
as closely as it deserves – and these are two modes of
underplaying – it is an outstanding demonstration of
affinity as well as attraction, of an embrace that hardly
requires any touching.

How was it on the sound stages at Paramount where
Sternberg was creating the exotic lighting patterns of
North Africa? He favoured Marlene, but must have

guessed already that she was too inherently promiscuous to stay loyal to his power of discovering or revealing her. Marlene knew what Sternberg was seeing – and
she would learn in time that other directors could not
get it, but she was far too given to common sense to
worship his refinement or grant it special privileges in
dealing with her. Ms Dietrich, it turned out, had a very
American attitude to being discovered. She reckoned
that – like chewing gum or the electric light – she
deserved everyone.

She liked to be laid. She was amused at how Lupe
Velez became possessive whenever Marlene passed by.
So she waited for the Mexican to wander and then
closed in on Cooper. Possessed by the same urge, and
seeing release as a practical duty, he was hardly likely to
be slow or discreet, especially when he had contempt
for the way Sternberg worked: talking in German, fuss-
ing with the lights to the detriment of the people, and
generally ignoring Tom Brown (as if Brown can be
understood). The two men fought and there is a story
that Coop once picked him up and shook him in an
effort to get him to be more sensible. Later on, Cooper
refused to work with Sternberg again – and it is more
than likely that Cooper never grasped the astonishing
sexual pirate Sternberg had recognized in him. Most of
his life Cooper preferred directors who were pals, good
guys and sports. Sternberg knew far too much about
human complexity to leave Cooper comfortable. (Henry
Hathaway – Cooper's type, and later the director of

seven of his films – was an assistant director on
Morocco.)

So *Morocco* 'made' Dietrich and yet it also established
Cooper. All the talk focused on her audacity and the dar-
ing departures in the character of Amy Jolly. But what
the film also – without effort or thought or reflection –
endorsed was the superb, nihilistic self-possession of
the largely silent Brown. He had slipped through – and
I think it's true that Sternberg never again allowed such
authority to a male character. Of course, there was
an obscure bargain in the film, very flattering to the
American man: that while continental films might have
sophisticated ideas and reckless ways of behaving, these
amounted to mere waves at the feet of an unbridled
American male presence. The film was fatuous, perhaps, but it left the male confidence in charge. And so
the legend built that Cooper said very little because he
had an inner resolve, a knowledge and an integrity that
did not need to stoop to talk. Don't explain, don't complain – it is a code that you can find in Hemingway as
easily as in John Wayne or Clint Eastwood. And while
Wayne was working already, he was not established
in pictures until the late '30s. Cooper led the way as
a potently quiet man in talking pictures. To this very
day – on screen and in private life – Clint Eastwood
practises the same economy, and has grown rich on it.

And then, suddenly, a spasm of anxiety went through
the noble tree. He was working hard at something where

he was famous for lack of apparent effort — but that does not mean that the outlay of nervous energy was modest. Paramount sometimes had him doing two films at a time, one by day and the other by night. He lost as much as thirty pounds, it was said, despite his unrivalled appetite. Of course, he was as busy in private and it was easy to depict that sort of schedule as a young man's fantasy. But Frank Cooper — from Bedfordshire and Montana — was also thrown out of rhythm by all he had to do. Lupe Velez was a delightful companion most of the time, but she could be a hounding, driving force. Cooper's mother, Alice, was worried about him, and doctors advised a significant rest period. It's not exactly a Cooper scenario, or not one Legionnaire Tom Brown would have tolerated, but the guy pursued by women all for $7,000 a picture was falling apart. It is fit material for a Lubitsch comedy — and may explain why that great director was beginning to cast his eyes on Coop. The American womanizer — like Frank Flanagan from Billy Wilder's *Love in the Afternoon* — it's a tempting subject. A simple case of not getting enough sleep?

There's an interesting side-angle view on Cooper at this time. Cecil Beaton, the English photographer (and three years younger than Cooper), was in Hollywood shooting portraits of some of the famous people. He found the actor,

absolutely charming, very good looking with black eyelashes as the lower lid and on the upper. Very tall, a good figure and

such a good sort that he made one feel such a swine. He was
on such good terms with everyone. The electrician offered
him a cigar. "Are they all right?" "Well, they should be. The
three cost 25 cents." And so Gary lit up and the cigar did not
explode. He was extremely smartly dressed with a brown hat
to match his suit and gloves, very elaborate gloves with green
spots in the lining. He is just a very charming cowboy and it
was amusing to see him so smartly turned out. His success is
stupendous. He is about the most popular actor on the
screen, and is paid fabulous sums. It is an extraordinary phenomenon this suddenly leaping to fame, he has only been in
the business three years and now it saps him entirely. He
longs to get away, but can't – he can't spend his money even,
he longs for the sun to stop shining but it never does.

Later on, Beaton would say that he had Coop as a
lover, briefly, and here is a point at which one has to con-
cede the underground assertion that Gary Cooper –
like several other famous stars – had at least a bisexual
period. Don't underestimate how far the movies had
liberated all manner of fantasies – for the public, but
for the movie-makers, too. The sense of liberty and of
what George Cukor called a belle époque was extraordinary, and it deserves to be read into the comedies of
the period. There is no firm evidence, though there are
too many stories for the idea to die: Coop was beautiful
to men and women – and nature seldom resists beauty.

It seems likely that Cooper's mother took a hand, and
effectively directed her son. Alice Cooper was not fond

of Lupe Velez and she seems to have worked hard to end the relationship. She may even have taken the lead in sending her boy out of the country. Not long afterwards, Cooper spoke up for himself, without naming names, and said that he regretted letting others determine his life for him. We have hints only, but it's especially interesting in that it's so much at odds with the idea and the resplendent screen icon – the man who moved to his own music and no other. 'I shall never be dominated by other people again as I had allowed myself to be . . . Had drifted, taken advice, let people get at me through my emotions, my sympathy, my affections. Perhaps through a sort of apathy, too, because I was not well.'

In the spring of 1931, he took a boat to Algiers – it was as if, somehow, he was following the path of Amy Jolly. From there he moved on to Italy, by then nine years into its period of Fascist government, and that's how he met the Countess Dorothy di Frasso. It was the Hollywood producer Walter Wanger who got him to the princess's parties. Dorothy Taylor had been born in upstate New York in 1888 and had inherited $12 million from her father, who was in the leather goods business – a specialty of the house was gloves. In 1923 she married the Count Carlo Dentice di Frasso – a man thirty years her senior. Dorothy was attractive, fun and she was an expert rider – quite enough for Coop. She had a restored villa that was said to be the location of an ongoing party. Almost immediately, Cooper became

Dorothy's lover (or one of them), and one of the outstanding figures at her palace, the Villa Madama.

I think it's fair to suppose that she gave good value,
and did a lot to form the creature that would be Gary
Cooper for the rest of his life. She desired him, but had
no notion of marrying him: without that threat, good
sex can be highly educational. She introduced him to
society people (including Mussolini and Ben Siegel),
and she may have been an essential influence on his
dress code and his political attitudes. Coop was born to
wear clothes – not just handsome, he had a real physical
grace, and a true respect for looking sensational. His
dress was often casual in later life, but never other than
perfect. Above all, the Countess di Frasso may have
taught Cooper this great social lesson: that if a handsome man wants to sleep around, he needs to be discreet and he requires a beautiful wife. Of course, the
only extra ingredient in the survival recipe is a certain
dash of cynicism. That, too, she seems to have inspired
in him.

With or without the countess, Cooper travelled
extensively in his 'rest' period. They went to East Africa,
they did an extensive safari and they shot wild animals,
a sport at which Coop only proved his boyhood skills as
a marksman. Di Frasso, apparently, shot a great deal of
home movie of the trip, none of which now survives.
This is a tragedy for – whether in the day hunting, or at
evening in camp, taking a drink – Coop may have been
the iconographic model for a host of adventure films

(from *King Solomon's Mines* to *Out of Africa* – note that Hemingway's *Green Hills of Africa* was published in 1935; Cooper had been there two years ahead of the writer).

In the next few years, Cooper would be asked to imagine himself in uniform in the area of the Khyber Pass, as western heroes, as Marco Polo and even as a defender of a republican cause up in the mountains of Spain, taking a girl into his sleeping bag. It may be that Cooper needed to be naïve to imagine himself really there in those perilous locations, but East Africa was better practice than most adventure heroes in the movies had had. Cagney, Gable, Colman were studio guys, doing their best, but Cooper had done a version of the grand tour. A time would come, when Cooper met Ernest Hemingway – the spiritual father of the sportsman movie hero – and Papa would be impressed not just that the clothes looked good on Cooper, but that the one-time cowboy was a much better shot than the writer.

There is a photograph of Cooper on a ship coming back from East Africa in 1932 – he is burnished by the sun, nearly a blond, amazingly slender in striped singlet and a casual knockout. You don't need to be told that this fellow was probably taking as many of the women he met as he could, from a countess to a beautiful African. And you feel from the picture the confidence that Cooper had in himself, and that others felt in him – he is the hero; no inventing is needed. In 1932 and 33 there wasn't a man anywhere who managed to look so beautiful and so tough.

Within months of returning from this trip, Cooper met Veronica Balfe, his wife-to-be. She was barely twenty, the daughter of Veronica Gibbons and Harry Balfe, the son of a very wealthy Irishman who had made a fortune in the US. The parents' marriage was disastrous and after a divorce Veronica married Paul Shields, a big hit in brokerage on Wall Street and an important friend and adviser to Gary Cooper the actor. It should be added that Paul Shields, homely looking and very hard-working, was apparently a great ladies' man who counted Marilyn Monroe among his conquests. Which only indicates the common ground necessary to male friendships.

The younger Veronica was widely known as 'Rocky', in great part because she was an athlete and sportswoman. She was tall, dark and beautiful enough to entertain a movie career. But she had the best inside advice: her mother's brother was Cedric Gibbons, the Irish-born premier set designer at Metro-Goldwyn-Mayer and the husband to Dolores Del Rio (they married in 1930), the very beautiful Mexican actress. One way or another, Gibbons made it clear to Rocky that she was unlikely to succeed as an actress. Meanwhile, he introduced her to every young man he could think of.

As 'Sandra Shaw', Rocky seems to have had a bit part in a Cooper film – *Today We Live* – that ended on the cutting-room floor. She also had a moment in *King Kong*. It was around this time that she and Coop met, on Richard Barthelmess's yacht, going over to Catalina on a weekend, and by 15 December 1933 they were married. People who saw them together caught the matching handsomeness and their shared interest in sports, but they noticed the guy was by far the more shy and reserved, while Rocky spoke her mind like someone used to a lot of money and to being obeyed. She immediately wrapped up her acting career and became a Hollywood wife. As events would prove, that was not the smoothest of paths, but Rocky Cooper never quite lost her man and in his dying years she succeeded in getting him into her Catholic Church. She was married to a perfect man and a chronic sinner, and that can be hard. But she never gave up on him or made his weaknesses public.

The couple would build a large white house in Brentwood: it had ample gardens where Coop the farmer planted corn and fruit trees; there was a large garage for the actor's cherished cars; and a kennel building where they bred Sealyhams and boxers. In time, they had a daughter, Maria Veronica, born in 1938. She was raised as a Catholic and when it came to getting her into the 'right' Catholic school, Cooper submitted to a modest religious service to correct the fact that he and Rocky had not been married in the Church.

It was a happy marriage, in part because Rocky followed the policy of being 'number two' in public and never being seen to disagree with her husband. In private, she could be impatient with his long-winded way with a story, and it's likely that she believed in her own

Mr and Mrs Gary Cooper

superior faculties. Over the years, she took a lot, and there is usually some private way for anger to be expressed. Nearly anyone studying Coop's face as he ages sees the onset of guilt – though it's worth noting that the first time that look appeared on screen, in *Mr. Deeds Goes to Town* (1936), was when the marriage was new.

In the early 1930s, as an actor, Gary Cooper did whatever was asked of him. There's no evidence that he sought or manoeuvred for particular parts. He was miscast several times, by Paramount, but he did not seem to complain to anyone about it. He had gone into picture-making with the expressed attitude that he wasn't quite sure he was going to be able to carry it off, and somehow that canny modesty left him out of the blame if ever a picture failed. But it's clear at this stage that Paramount were a little confused over whether to emphasize the man of action or the romantic lead.

So there are oddities in his list of credits, which has to include the film of *A Farewell to Arms*. In hindsight, that looks like superb casting: who else should play the American soldier in Italy who loses faith with the Allied war effort and the sacred process of marriage, and who becomes an outsider as he pursues his tragic love affair with an English nurse? As you read Hemingway's prose, it is not hard to imagine that you see the film before you – with Cooper, say, and Margaret Sullavan, tough, fatalistic, with the love story allowed to speak for itself. But read the Hemingway again and you may begin to detect what a loaded male weepie it is – unless conceived and shot in ways that can show the love-making without the flowery talk that lays claim to it.

In other words, the kernel of Hemingway's story was such that certain things seen should outweigh any celebration of them in talk. But in 1932, the time of the film – even before the full onset of the Code – it was impossible for the production system to treat sex so candidly, or to have lovers step outside the tracks of patrotic duty and observance of the marriage codes. *A Farewell to Arms* needs to be what the title suggests – a moment when utter realism forces two lovers to guard their love in a collapsing world. But the Code could not condone collapse, and so every laconic sinew in Cooper – in Tom Brown a few years older – was forsaken in a high-gloss romantic style that made Hemingway wince.

The film was directed by Frank Borzage who was not just expert, but heartfelt, with stories of frustrated or separated lovers and of romantic idylls sustained in grim times. The actress was Helen Hayes – a stage star – who did her best but who never achieves the kind of intensity that Frederick and Catherine enjoy in the book. Whenever possible, Borzage sought 'uplift' to temper the realism – so there's a showy first-person shot of Frederick being taken into the operating theatre, and there's a secret marriage ceremony to appease moral guardians. Above all, Borzage and Paramount felt they were filming a 'great story', whereas the one left by Hemingway is ordinary yet fateful. *A Farewell to Arms* was nominated for Best Picture, but that was a courtesy to its inspirational pretensions and to the still hopeless gap that existed between literary directness and movie dreaming. There was no reason to blame Cooper. He looked splendid, even if he seemed to have no sure idea as to what the picture was about.

Cooper was loaned out to Metro-Goldwyn-Mayer for *Today We Live* – his first encounter with Howard Hawks. It was a war story, scripted by William Faulkner from his short story, 'Turn About', and intended to star Gable. But when Gable could not fit it in his schedule, Hawks went to Cooper. It was then that the modest actor apparently told MGM that he was about to appear in a very considerable film – *A Farewell to Arms* – and he negotiated his bonus up from $13,000 to $20,000. All Metro begged in return was that a part be found for Joan Crawford. The picture flopped, but it's watchable, and there is a chemistry between Cooper and Crawford like real stars recognizing each other.

At which point, Paramount took on *Design for Living*, the Noël Coward play which had been a big stage hit, starring Alfred Lunt, Lynn Fontanne and Coward himself. Yet again, the studio was hoping to purchase literary prestige by denying itself all the risqué things that had worked on stage – essentially the idea of a *ménage à trois* in operation. The threesome were Gary Cooper, Fredric March and Miriam Hopkins – and Cooper certainly proved his ability to wear good clothes. With equal insouciance, the same year Paramount thrust

Cooper into their all-star production of *Alice in Wonderland* – and asked him to play the White Knight.

Stranger still was *Operator 13* in which Marion Davies played a Union spy during the American Civil War. Much of the time she is in blackface disguise – until she meets a charming Confederate officer played by Gary Cooper. Davies was four years older than Cooper, and her acting career was nearly over: *Operator 13* was the kind of nonsense that ruined her. The most likely reason for Cooper's presence was that he and Rocky had been guests at Hearst Castle and were anxious not to lose this social connection. But there was a bonus to *Operator 13*, for it was on that picture that Cooper met Jack Moss, the man who would become his manager.

It is not that Cooper had ever been cheated by the system. Somehow, the reluctant and inarticulate cowboy cleaned up. Those who knew him well declared that the famous manner masked but did not kill his enormous desire for money. In 1932 he had earned $85,000, and in 1933 the figure climbed to $133,000. But that was preparation for the campaigning by Jack Moss and his father-in-law, Paul Shields. The quality of the films improved and Coop's earnings accelerated: $258,000 in 1934; $328,000 in 1935; $370,000 in 1937; and $482,000 in 1939. By then, Cooper was among the highest paid people in America. Moreover, he took advice and invested money in land – in Montana, but in Californa, too. He had an early ownership in land that eventually became Palm Springs airport. This is the method behind the real movie fortunes: take lowly taxed income and convert it to property. And this, in fact, is the real mindset behind the very winning but rather far-fetched attitude of Longfellow Deeds, irked and restricted by the $20 million he inherits and inclined to give away as much of it as he can.

So as I praise *Mr. Deeds Goes to Town* (and, warts and all, it is better than what Cooper had been doing in the early '30s), we need to respect the attendant ironies. Just like Frank Capra, his director, Gary Cooper was an assiduous and even neurotic banker of his own funds. And now, he seemed more persuaded that better choices of material would boost those funds.

Now and Forever is a Shirley Temple film, but one that presents a new facet of Gary Cooper. He plays a rogue, a confidence trickster, working in Paris, while his wife's family looks after the little girl left motherless. Moreover, the father is prepared to relinquish his hold on the child for cash in hand. But then they meet and charm gets to work. The five-year-old girl and the cowboy get along. Coop goes down on his knees for her. He buys her presents and draws pictures for her. The film is routine, but Cooper's openness to the child is neither coy nor contrived. It's as if he's found a kindred spirit. Indeed, he seems more interested in her than he does in Carole Lombard (who plays his second wife). Cooper had a fling with Lombard but she didn't really like him – she thought he was languid and even effeminate.

In its conclusion, *Now and Forever* takes several unexpected directions. Yet the father is redeemed, if not excused, and the way in which he faces his own charming weakness as a man is worthy of a far better picture. But it's a myth to think that Shirley Temple made childish pictures. In so many ways she was grown up, and so often her films ask a great deal of the adults.

Quite early in their marriage, Gary and Rocky Cooper became favoured guests at the Goldwyn house — often in foursomes where dinner was followed by bridge. It was the start of a momentous association, the move that would alter Cooper's status in Hollywood. Of course, Goldwyn had hankered after Cooper ever since *The Winning of Barbara Worth*, and he was given to lamenting the way in which he had let the cowboy get away.

So Goldwyn asked if perhaps he could borrow Coop for one film. Goldwyn had brought a beautiful young actress from Russia — Anna Sten — and he was close to despair over trying to make an international star of her. He would try one last time, with *The Wedding Night*, in which Cooper would play a successful young novelist living in the country and Sten was the Polish girl who buys land from him. Cooper said he'd do the picture for $150,000, and Paramount agreed. King Vidor was set to direct.

Very soon, he hit trouble: Vidor had it in mind to make the picture about the clash of urban and rural society, but the studio wanted the romance emphasized — hence the rather overbearing title. Moreover, it was Vidor's hope to make Cooper fit the mould of a Scott Fitzgerald type of novelist. This never worked, and it led to two hesitant speakers seeking to get the other one to go first. Sten lacked the humour to make the stand-off work, and the film was a warning for Goldwyn, though one that he declined to notice. Sten's career was over, so once more no one sought to give Gary Cooper any of the responsibility. Back at Paramount, he hit a run of films that are all directly associated with his stardom: *The Lives of a Bengal Lancer*; *Peter Ibbetson*; and *Desire*.

The Lives of a Bengal Lancer makes uncomfortable viewing today; we are transported to the general area of the Khyber Pass (or the best views of it available in the Californian Sierra), yet we are asked to behold traditional attitudes to the peoples there in a way that surely begins to explain why they might now despise us and seek to destroy us. Is their venturing forth to Manhattan, say, any more intrusive than the notion that the British needed forts and garrisons and pig-sticking contests in the old North-West Frontier? What was being protected, beyond a certain schoolboy attitude?

But *The Lives of a Bengal Lancer* has its code: there are two seasoned soldiers (Gary Cooper and Franchot Tone, and they make quite a nice sparring partnership), plus the novice, the kid, Richard Cromwell, who is also the son of the colonel (played by Sir Guy Standing, an aristocratic actor). The Code says that this colonel cannot recognize his son as a son, only as a subaltern. That

barrier inspires the whole story, for the two more seasoned lancers are so intent on protecting the emotion-
ally inept father that they will do anything to save him
from knowing about his son's cowardice when faced by
torture – the torture is that of burning bamboo splints
thrust beneath the fingernails, and Cooper handles this
assault like a man with a nasty ulcer.

Of course, *The Lives of a Bengal Lancer* is a classic – all
the way to Cooper's sacrificial death for which he gets
the Victoria Cross. There may have been young would-
be officers in 1935 who took heart from its brisk nonsense and felt their ethnic superiority armoured by the
way Douglas Dumbrille and Monte Blue represent
suave, cruel and utterly empty barbarians (who somehow speak good English). The action is well handled (by
Henry Hathaway). There is a quite amusing sequence
with a cobra as well as the clear antecedent for such
films to come as *Beau Geste*, *The Four Feathers* and *Gunga
Din*. It is certainly one of the films that Cooper's male
audience most cherished. The greatest shock may come
in learning that it was also nominated as Best Picture.

Whereas, *Peter Ibbetson* is a film that may still need to
be properly appreciated. It is from a novel by George
Du Maurier, published in 1891 and inspired by dream
experiences and by the Heloise and Abelard story. Two
people meet and fall in love as children. Years later, they
re-encounter by chance, but no sooner have they realized what they mean to each other than he is caught up
in a killing that leads to his being jailed. It is a matter of

critical insight that many great movie love stories – in whole or in part – involve separation of the lovers. A final embrace may suffice for standard fare. But the intrinsic nature of the screen (cross-cut close-ups) and of movie-going (us in the dark separated from them in the light) makes yearning and separation the most potent forces. Of course, this is somewhat at odds with an audience and a business greedy for embraces, and more. But there is also the Romantic ideal that a love unrealized is eternal. *Peter Ibbetson* is one of the very few films to address that issue directly.

It is nearly a matter for comedy that it should be directed by Henry Hathaway, just out of the saddle of a Bengal lancer! How much the subject seems to cry out for Buñuel or Vigo or Mizoguchi. To which some might add that Gary Cooper and Ann Harding are both a little too earthbound for these lovers who live like clouds in dream's sky. So you do your best and in the best case, I would argue, reach the conclusion that *Peter Ibbetson* is a very peculiar film to come out of Paramount in 1935. In period clothes and periodic speech, Cooper seems far from comfortable. But in this inevitable study of gaze, it does emerge that he has a watchful, thinking face – he is accustomed to seeing the unseen, the imaginary.

Romance cannot endure too much togetherness. At the end of *Desire*, Tom Bradley (Cooper) and Madeleine de Beaupre (Marlene Dietrich) are apparently headed for Detroit – his town and the place where their love will turn into family and Grosse Pointe. It is a playful mercy in the picture that *Desire* doesn't get to Detroit, though the inquisitive among us may hunger to see that sequel. Isn't it wiser that Tom and Madeleine's love stays linked yet fenced off, too, by that string of pearls rather than go crazy in Detroit?

You see, in *Desire* they are a pert movie couple. No matter how extreme and logical Cooper and Dietrich seemed in *Morocco*, no one wanted to miss their reunion in a film produced by Ernst Lubitsch and plainly conceived of by him, but actually directed by Frank Borzage. It's not that *Desire* is neglected, but still it is a far better film than the general estimate allows. Even Graham Greene's opinion – that it was the best film Dietrich had made in America – bears examination.

Tom is lyrically happy in his job – indeed, he is sometimes prompted to start singing about the car he helped design, the Bronson. He is in Paris now (don't ask why) finishing the job and on his vacation he is allowed to drive the Bronson into a Spain that has not yet been told about its civil war. Meanwhile, Madeleine has played the leading role in stealing an exquisite string of pearls. They meet on the road and then again at the customs post at the border. Anticipating search, Madeleine slips the pearls (about the weight and size of a mature cobra) into Tom's jacket pocket. That entrance, a very Lubitschian touch, is as delightfully sexual as every theft in Bresson's *Pickpocket*.

Well, does she have trouble getting the pearls back! But is life made easier and more complicated by the fact that Tom falls in love with her? Bradley is one of Coop's most engaging chumps – effortlessly gorgeous, helplessly optimistic, brilliant on cars but boyish in most other matters. This film was famously Dietrich's escape from Sternberg and I think we can see Lubitsch taking extra pleasure in showing us, truly, how adorable, warm, tender and down-to-earth Marlene can be. She has one of her songs in the film – 'Awake in a Dream', by Friedrich Hollaender – but she sings it not with the acid flourish that accompanies the numbers in Sternberg films, but entirely simply, like someone in a Jacques Demy movie. I'm not sure she ever looked more beautiful, but I'm sure that the rich language of looks, nudges, sighs and simperings she and Cooper worked out (he does most of the simperings) was one of the several stages in American film that made an ass of the Hays Code. *Morocco* is a main course, if you like, but here is a serious dessert. As Steven Bach put it, 'This kind of chemistry appears only rarely in a decade, and makes sense of the whole star system.'

Desire was shot in the fall of 1935, when the Cooper marriage was coming up on two years old. To appreciate the test on that marriage fully, you have to know how to read a look. And the way Coop and Marlene gaze at each other in the film might have sent a less stern or solemn world headlong to depravity, let alone Detroit. This is liquid sex added to film emulsion, the most fragrant, sticky black and white anyone could wish for. It establishes that the American man was very vulnerable to feminine sophistication, and by all rights it should have dissolved the prospects for male courage and brute strength in America. But there was a war coming so we must make allowances. What Rocky Cooper made of it is another matter. I will stake my credentials as a film observer on the conclusion that the two stars were delighting in each other – or putting on an act likely to drive a wife mad, unless she could find an official way of not looking. Needless to say, Cooper got paid for this – a mere $93,000 – but he never manages to look as if screwed, no matter that Marlene got $200,000.

Longfellow Deeds from Mandrake Falls in Vermont: the name and address are one of those attempts at Americana and archetypalism that Frank Capra brought to American film of the 1930s. But 'Longfellow' does not quite match the creative mischief of *Desire* where Madeleine at one point estimates the size of America, with a wistful look in her eyes, as 'Six foot three'. Nevertheless, *Mr. Deeds Goes to Town* is one of the handful of best-known films Gary Cooper ever made – *Mr. Deeds, Sergeant York, Pride of the Yankees, For Whom the Bell Tolls, High Noon*. Five great guys, but each one deserving a pinch of salt – and a dab of mustard.

Mr. Deeds Goes to Town is still honoured as an American classic: it was nominated for Best Picture; it won a second directing Oscar for Frank Capra; and it won Cooper's first acting nomination (he lost to Paul Muni playing

Dr Pasteur). It was very popular and it established Capra's unique populism as a mood to restore morale after the worst years of the Depression. It remains highly entertaining, but I think its politics and its economics require careful scrutiny, just as anyone following Coop's career must note the considerable addition of gloom and anxiety. For the first time in his screen career, he seems haunted by the things he cannot articulate.

The premise is simple: Longfellow Deeds lives in Mandrake Falls in faraway Vermont. He has a hobby – the tuba – and a job: writing the verse for greeting cards. When we first see him, in Vermont, he is Coop, to be sure – lanky, independent, apparently oblivious to women or the world, just honking along on the tuba. Well, through a very distant relationship he inherits $20 million, for which, he knows, he has no pressing need. So he plans to give the money away, on the principle that he neither earned nor deserved this windfall – and others have much more need for it.

It is characterisic of Capra, I would argue, that this sentiment is sentimentally appealing in great part because it ignores the political logic that lurks behind it. Like some real politicians from Vermont, Mr Deeds could be brought to his senses by the spectacle of a large packet of capital (or pork) going into undeserving hands. He could begin to muster a political point of view that argues for the reallocation of resources according to fairness (I apologize for being so bluntly offensive). The mere hint of so much socialism led to

the film being rejoiced at in Soviet Russia. But Capra
never goes that far: Deeds remains the eccentric individual, never the political test. Indeed, the loneliness
of his action is part and parcel of his Vermontism (as
Capra sees it). Vermont, in fact (I have lived there), is
a splendid, tough-minded liberal place. But Capra's
Vermont is a caricature of soft backwoods, rural cunning and an attitude that is content to let the world's
issues pass by. It is more a Sleepy Hollow than a state
in the union. So Deeds' generosity is neither logical
nor committed – it is quirky, and Coop is encouraged
to play the part as someone who is already not quite
right in the head. Notice how, even hearing the big
news from the visiting lawyers, he plays away on the
tuba. People in Vermont are not like that – they can
get excited over money, sex and sport (just like the
chumps in New Hampshire).

So the parable slips away from being a true model of
what America might do and becomes a cautionary tale
as to whether Deeds is a mere dreamer or waiting to be
locked up by the cops (that's where Jean Arthur comes
in as a snappy journalist who satirizes Deeds even as
she begins to fall in love with him – it was a shining
example in '30s comedy that good-natured mockery
was so often the path to love). And that is how the
movie ends in a weird tribunal to judge Deeds' sanity.
Moreover, the film has many moments when we see
that Deeds is so much off on his private track, so deeply
affected by rural obscurity, that he is not in our world.

There are shots of Coop, staring out of his window, fixed in melancholy, which show the admixture of iso-lation and self-pity that so often prevents Capra heroes from the hard thinking they need to do. And the Coo-per who was so alert in *Desire* is now half-asleep.

Of course, it all turns out fine: Capra was afraid of unhappy endings or unresolved energies. But his social parables also depend on sighting but not really hitting the nervous system of the nation. No one is truly offended or threatened, and the idea of giving away your money (or pooling our resources) is obscured by the feeble question of whether Longfellow is a simple-ton or not. That's where Cooper's droll, dry presence is so elastic, and so different from his earlier films. But Capra was so discerning a director he could see that Cooper's face was ready to yield close-ups of great anguish and distress – as the farmer recounts how hard the hard times are, and as the innocent kindness of a Deeds becomes tangled in human mockery. Make no mistake, neither Capra nor Cooper endorsed the idea in *Deeds* of the social use of resources and capital. But they colluded in the pretty masquerade of social respon-sibility. And in making his film with such skill, Capra uncovered and fostered a brooding disquiet in Gary Cooper – a mood that was to affect him more and more (perhaps it seemed like acting) as he became steadily richer, more isolated and more selfish in his private actions.

Of course, the Cooper–Capra story was only just

begun: *Meet John Doe* is a more rueful, wounding picture by far, and one that easily accommodates and shackles Cooper's athletic nature and his optimistic demeanour. *Mr. Deeds* is still a tricky film to handle, and I am not minimizing Capra's cleverness – it was close to miraculous to make a Hollywood film that even questioned the leverage of capital. But it bears close watching, and it is in tracking Cooper that the dangers are most painful. As Pauline Kael said, 'Frank Capra destroyed Gary Cooper's early sex appeal when he made him childish as Mr Deeds. Cooper, once devastatingly lean and charming, the man Tallulah and Marlene had swooned over, began to act like an old woman and went on to a long sexless career – fumbling, homey, mealy-mouthed.' 'Old woman' is harsh, I feel, but Kael was sharpest when disappointed in love.

It's because Deeds feels like a victim, caught in an unfair trap, that this neutering begins. Who knows how far a new wife's reproach was also urging Gary to be less overtly sexy or attractive on screen? It is one of the great mysteries in Hollywood, but it also helps the creation of a stalwart image to cover up the real promiscuity and irresponsibility of the man. In many Hollywood careers there comes an awkward moment when a man or woman decides to be more likeable – and time and again it betrays the shallowness and insecurity of their thinking.

It's only fair to mention the praise *Mr. Deeds* received and still receives. The film moves people, and it does raise the idea of a society, its resources and the humane use of them. Graham Greene, writing from England, thought the film a huge success where the happy ending arose naturally from the material. (Greene was hardsoft in his own endings.) He was not as struck by the diminution in Cooper's robust attitudes. For Greene, Capra 'believes in the possibility of happiness; he believes in spite of the controlling racketeers, in human nature. Goodness, simplicity, disinterestedness: these in his hands become fighting qualities. Deeds sees though opera directors, fashionable intellectuals, solicitors, psychologists who prove that he is insane merely because he likes playing the tuba and isn't greedy for money.' And Greene felt that Coop's 'subtle and pliable performance' was perfect and a great advance.

For myself, I find *Mr. Deeds* sentimentally clammier and more frustrating as the years pass. I think Kael has detected a crucial failing in the extra burden of soulful and rather pious ordinariness on Longfellow Deeds, and he has wrapped that up in a view of Vermont that never matches my impression of a green and intelligent state that can easily reckon it leads America – as opposed to being an idyllic but becalmed Rip Van Winkle retreat. You have to see the film to reach your own conclusion. In which case, let's settle for the moment on the relatively easy ground that *Mr. Deeds Goes to Town* is a problem picture and a turning point in the life of Gary Cooper.

*   *   *

The General Died at Dawn could hardly begin better. We see the streets of ruined towns, with corpses on the ground and dark birds of prey circling in the air (one seems to dance on a string). We see Chinese troops marching through long blond grasses. We feel the heat of the sun and our own complete ignorance of China. It is a time of 'harsh warlords', a cliché that has given rise to Akim Tamiroff, late of the Moscow Arts Theatre, but now masquerading as the very wicked General Yang. Who knows why or how, but Yang is having hard times as a vicious warlord: he is short of money and his troops are deserting him. Thus there appears a white man named O'Hara, an adventurer, a mercenary and a fashion plate.

He wears a fedora hat cast down over one eye, a checked shirt with a single-coloured tie in a much lighter material. He has a raincoat not buttoned up, but loosely tied across his waist in a way that shows his belt buckle. He also wears riding boots, and in one pocket of his coat he has a monkey, his pet and his pal. It is a very arresting first appearance and an important example in the progress Gary Cooper was making as a clothes horse. The costumes on the picture are credited to Travis Banton (who is more generally associated with women's clothes and salons in the better part of town). So it's possible that Cooper simply dressed himself. Still, it's a question that we linger over in that the simple if unlikely appearance of O'Hara – the confluence of the dandified and the casual – is by far the most interesting thing about this fatuous picture.

You can argue that someone at Paramount recollected Sternberg's *Shanghai Express*, and dreamed of remaking it. You can conjecture that the lifelong playwright Clifford Odets (beacon of the Group Theatre and engaged on his first screenplay with a zeal that should have been taken as a warning) was somehow drawn to a kind of civil war story that might be thought to be modelled on Spain and which offered the chance of so many dire speeches on liberty et cetera. Maybe those opening shots of a 'Chinese' landscape promised a picture with military skirmishing and a modest amount of massacre. It's not too hard to credit that this eccentrically dressed O'Hara is really a good warrior in republican causes who seeks to bring peace, gentleness and the Olympic Games to China. Or you could settle for the equally persuasive idea that, in 1936, no one in Hollywood knew anything about or was interested in China as anything except a place where 'intrigue' might reign, along with the chance for Moscow Arts Theatre actors to wear lurid make-up scars and hiss out baleful lines in pidgin English.

It is worse than that. It is nonsense, wearying to follow, quite wasteful of an intriguing iconographic resemblance between Cooper and his female lead, Madeleine Carroll, and unfairly neglectful of one interesting speech she confides to the camera on how she has the blues and there ought to be a law against such things (or opium). Instead, the script has her betray O'Hara in the intrigue – it's a matter of his money-belt that is the key to the local political future – so that she must redeem herself after he has slapped her pretty forcefully in the face (this gesture is arresting but disconcerting in that it suggests O'Hara has a turmoil of mixed feelings about the girl, whereas the movie itself reveals nothing of the kind – Coop does not often do mixed feelings).

You take it for granted that the film will get out-of-doors very soon, but no – like someone with a bad cold it stays indoors (in fact, Carroll's father does have a silly, nagging cough which I fear is meant to convey moral decay). The inertia may owe a lot to the pretensions of Odets who generally felt that movies were lucky if they came under his reforming intelligence. In fact, this one grinds to a halt and gets itself into a warren of competing directions. There is no action, no suspense, there is not even a moment where the monkey takes a bullet to save O'Hara (though there is the real John O'Hara – the writer, seen briefly on a train – and spoken to by Cooper as a numbing touch of 'reality').

The film is directed by Lewis Milestone and it leaves one amazed by whatever has happened to that once significant name – after all, the picture has 'China', a money-belt, a monkey, Cooper and Carroll (who seem to grasp their basic duty of gazing at each other). It has Tamiroff, with a cruel glee made to behold the victims of slow torture. How could something more engrossing not emerge? How was the picture completed? And how does it have any kind of reputation?

For the sentimental purposes of this book, it would

be nice to be able to say that *The General Died at Dawn* has slipped into unfair neglect whereas the neglect only shows the sanity of the nation and the widespread understanding of what a good picture used to be. Still, inasmuch as it is far from alone in Cooper's credits, this picture does testify to just how much erosion or self-erasure Coop could survive. It is as if people only remembered that louche first appearance and the way the monkey comes out of the raincoat pocket. It's as if that handsome stiff was so adorable and so trusted as a hero that he could survive this kind of nonsense. Surely anyone really watching Cooper could have seen *Morocco*, *Desire* and *Mr. Deeds* and seen what a remarkable fellow this was – and then the studio orders him into this chinoiserie as if they saw no difference. And who is to say that Coop himself could tell the difference? Other actors in this series did have a feeling for their own material – Bogart and Bette Davis, say – and spoke out, got suspended and ended up in court to make manifest their feeling that they deserved better. Coop, on the other hand, hardly deviates in his stroll. He seemed so taken aback that others in charge should trust him as an actor, let alone an attraction, that he had decided he didn't have the heart to offend anyone.

I have omitted one thing of possible value. O'Hara gets shot in the course of the action. There is a wound in his side that has to be treated. Off comes his shirt, and in goes the iodine – or whatever. Am I crazy or don't you feel the very film stock tense up a little? At long last this silly film has itself a side of reliable spectacle and a chest over which some might dream. Suddenly the screen is filled with meat or with a mesa-like land formation such as can take your breath away in a Western. I do not raise this point lightly (though Milestone was not the man to pursue it), but grant this impact and the terrific panache of O'Hara in his first costume and I think I'd have dropped a lot of the Odets talk (hear it falling, like a log delivery) and settled for a film about a man dressing and undressing. It only shows how in the 1930s a little maleness could go a long way.

Cecil B. DeMille had been operating for most of his life as an independent and successful producer on the slopes of the Paramount mountain. He must have seen Gary Cooper all the time and wondered about him. Then, in 1936, he was taken with the idea of a new, bold type of Western. DeMille had done the Western before, in two versions of *The Squaw Man*. But he had not really harnessed the genre to his brazen and scary view of America's destiny as the great subject that faced religion in an irreligious age. And so he approached *The Plainsman*.

Like most DeMille films, this one stirred known history until it was lost in the furious whirl. It begins in Washington, where a sad-looking Abraham Lincoln is urging his cabinet to consider the West as a fit emptying ground for all the country's demobilized soldiers and all its still armed dreams. Then he has to stop discussions to go to the theatre.

Whereupon, we switch locales violently – to the Dakotas, the Black Hills and the terrain where Buffalo Bill Cody and Wild Bill Hickok were friends, and Calamity Jane was their tomboy pal. They did meet; Hickok acted briefly for Cody in what would be the Wild West Show. But who's to know or care in America? And who's to worry when *The Plainsman* admits at the outset that it has conflated and rearranged events to help a movie along?

The Plainsman was directed by DeMille (with such vigour that you marvel at the way a Milestone had reputation still) and it was written by Waldemar Young, Lynn Riggs and Harold Lamb, and possibly others. The background to the film is the attempt by rascally traders (led by Charles Bickford – a scowl on legs) to sell guns to the Indians. The Indians, I should say, are treated favourably enough: they are savage, bloodthirsty and stupid, but they are clearly wronged and exploited, and unaccustomed to dialogue. They number among their tribes Anthony Quinn (DeMille's son-in-law). Cody and Hickok must do what they can to prevent war with the Indians and bring the rascals to justice. But, along the way, Custer does get shipped out and, of course, in a neat return to history in 1876 at the close of the film, Wild Bill is shot in the back by that rat-like coward and gambler Jack McCall (played by Porter Hall, the villain from *The General Died at Dawn*).

This was a big picture for 1936, when Westerns were not in plentiful supply – it ran 110 minutes. Gary

Cooper was Hickok. And the picture is still strangely moving.

How is that so? First and most important, Hickok has been made a character that Oscar Wilde might have cherished – not just a gambler-hero, but a rare fatalist, locked in a dark, edgy and ironic view of life, in love with Calamity Jane (Jean Arthur) but desperate not to admit it to her or to himself. He diverts his romantic energies into an obsession with clothes.

Every surviving picture of Hickok shows a stoat with long, dirty hair. The film will not let Cooper follow that image. His hair is longer than usual, and a little wavy, but it is quite clear that – wherever he is on the old prairie – he has access to a high-class barber's saloon every day. He is shaved and laundered. He is groomed. And he dresses in character – that's not a casual remark, for there is almost the sense that his dress code is not just external. It is philosophical. It is inward. It is a part of his gloomy wit, and it is a sign of distinction and indifference to the general uncouthness that affects most of the other men in this West. At first, he wears gorgeous light-toned buckskins with tasselled fringes (the sort of thing you'd have to go to Las Vegas for today), along with very elegant flat-brimmed, low-crowned hats. But then as the film advances, he settles increasingly for black, head to toe, with black boots and black hats. You can say this is DeMille teasing the old adage that in Westerns the good guys wore white hats – so Hickok is ambiguous. But it's far more than that. It's quite simply that in the primitive and early West one guy has found the wit and the nerve to dress inventively for every occasion. Here, as never quite before, is the grave beauty of the lean Coop doing no more than walk across the frame – for an eye that knows he is as handsome as the Grand Canyon.

Better still, this taste or tastefulness has reached out to Calamity Jane. At first, she is a roughhouse girl, but as time goes by her costumes improve just as Jean Arthur's make-up comes to be as complete as Anthony Quinn's warpaint. Thus there is a long passage where she wears a satin dress, all set against Bill's black. There's even the amazing erotic moment – and DeMille loved sex – where she shrugs off the lower part of the dress to reveal riding clothes underneath. Nothing in the books suggests there was an affair between Cooper and Arthur. But everything on screen sighs at its fragrance. Next to *Deeds*, the love story here has heat and a strange impact on composition – time and again the two people are pushed extra close together in odd, mannered ways that seem to address unspoken (or unspeakable?) needs.

As a matter of fact, Mae West had been DeMille's first thought for Jane and he had to forbid Jean Arthur from cropping her hair and looking tough. This is not just a new kind of Western, it is a sexy Western. And when Bill is shot dead it is nothing less than tragic. It doesn't matter that the real Calamity could have been named after her dishevelled looks. We feel the loss as one of the sad songs of the West. Moreover, Cooper spends the entire film doing things so small you wonder at first if you really saw them. DeMille has a reputation still for rawness and vulgarity, but this is a delicate, refined film, and it leaves one in no doubt about how the West was won – men and women fucked, and there was nothing plain about it and nothing that could impede it.

The Plainsman was a huge hit, and with *Deeds* it established Cooper as an American hero. Yet notice how far apart Hickok and Deeds are, and see how the fatalism in the Western makes for a muscular optimism and spirit while Deeds is nearly buried in his own self-pity. It is in 1936 that Cooper breaks into the top ten at the American box office, an event that stimulates a great change in his career and its management.

Gary and Rocky Cooper were still exploring no trumps with Sam and Frances Goldwyn. But card-play can be a cover for real talk. So, at one point, Cooper revealed the unbelievable – that Paramount were being so slow about renewing his contract it looked as if they might have forgotten it. In those days, of course, an employer could keep a contract player for ever, so long as he renewed every option and kept the money coming. Paramount had no thought of losing Cooper. They seem to have taken him for granted, and thus they left exposed a small window of opportunity in which he was engaged to no one. Well aware of the sharp practice, Goldwyn proposed a contract of his own for

Cooper whereby the actor was to do one picture a year for $150,000.

There were furious consequences. Paramount charged Goldwyn with interference. They thought that Cooper had behaved badly. But in the end there was nothing they could do about it. A Paramount renewal was duly negotiated, but the Goldwyn contract was untouchable – likely because Sam had asked for just one picture a year. And so Coop's salary went over $400,000 a year. Together, these two deals gave him rare power, but think what it would have been like if the films at Goldwyn had been any good.

The Adventures of Marco Polo was a project Goldwyn had taken over from Douglas Fairbanks Sr – in other words, it had been around for years. Robert Sherwood had written a script meant to be funny, and even anachronistic. This was the story of Polo, bringing the Western taste for kissing to China, in return for the discoveries of pasta and gunpowder. (You see how tidy history can be.) Nearly seventy-five years later, 'we' know no more and no less about Marco Polo – and we are still waiting for a good movie about him. However excited he may have been by the new deal with Goldwyn, Cooper was horrified by the script. He disliked lavish costume. He flinched from too much talk. And he didn't get the joke. Repeatedly he tried to get himself off the picture. One director, John Cromwell, resigned. Another, William Wyler, ducked the assignment. And so the film was shot with Archie Mayo in charge and Sigrid Gurie, a Norwegian actress, playing the Chinese princess. Basil Rathbone was the villain. Somehow or other, this misguided venture was allowed to cost $2 million and Goldwyn was said to have lost $700,000 on the one picture. At Paramount, that news was greeted with glee. For Cooper it rolled off his back like slippery spaghetti.

It's a marvel that Paramount didn't rebuke Cooper. Just as one has to wonder at the public's tolerance. In the late '30s, while climbing as a box-office favourite, Cooper did the following: *Souls at Sea* for Paramount, a sailing adventure in which Cooper felt himself outshone by George Raft; *The Adventures of Marco Polo*, for Goldwyn; back to Paramount for *Bluebeard's Eighth Wife*, a Lubitsch picture and a very sophisticated comedy; to Goldwyn for *The Cowboy and the Lady*, with Merle Oberon; back to Paramount for *Beau Geste*; and to Goldwyn for *The Real Glory*, an adventure film set in the early history of the Philippines, with Cooper playing a valiant doctor.

What's striking about that group, I fear, is that only one film – *Bluebeard's Eighth Wife* – really repays attention now. In part that comes from the way Lubitsch employed a new writing team – that of Billy Wilder and Charles Brackett – and then in turn their response to the subject of sexual frustration. Bluebeard, or Michael Brandon (Cooper), is a tycoon of business affairs and a collector of romantic liaisons. He has been married seven times as the picture opens. He meets number eight (Claudette Colbert) when the two of them bump into each other looking for matching halves of a pair of pyjamas. They marry, but that's when she plays hard to get. The film is not much cherished by the fans of Lubitsch, but I think it has a dark, Wilderian edge – a nastiness, even – that is uncommon. It's a film about marriage, feminism and frustration and one that rubs against the sexual confidence or complacency of Coop. Yes, it might be more – it might be the handsome lug going crazy with sexual denial. But it's a film full of perverse ideas and so much more interesting than, say, *The General Died at Dawn* or *The Cowboy and the Lady*.

Or even *Beau Geste*? Is it really sacrilege to challenge this chestnut among Foreign Legion films? Unfortunately, readers of this book and followers of Coop have their Foreign Legion picture already – *Morocco*, which is tougher-minded than all the sadism of Sergeant Markov (Brian Donlevy) in *Beau Geste*.

This is the story of *Beau Geste*. One day in the Sahara, a military patrol comes upon Fort Zinderneuf, an adobe fortress next to an oasis. The battlements seem manned, but in fact the men leaning over the parapet are all dead. A bugler goes forward to study the situation – it's Robert Preston, one of three Geste brothers who joined the Foreign Legion together. Why? Oh, because of the scandal at Brandon Abbas about the theft of the Blue Water sapphire, which had to be sold to pay the family debts – but no one could admit to that. It's the hell of being honourable and English and it all comes from the novel by P. C. Wren, published in 1924 and first filmed in '26 with Ronald Colman as 'Beau'.

But first there must be flashbacks to childhood (where Donald O'Connor is the young Beau, with ears you could fly a plane on) and then when they are young men. The silliness of the story is rivalled only by the stupidity of the Foreign Legion as an escape for these besmirched squires (nearly Wren's title, it seems). It also means that we don't see Gary Cooper in the desert until about forty minutes into the picture. And at that point Brian Donlevy's exultantly vicious Markov begins to steal the show. Indeed, it is his mad idea to put dead men in the gun-places to make the Touaregs feel that their mission (their whole life) is hopeless – as I recall, the Touaregs have not a single line of dialogue.

Beau Geste is ridiculous, no matter that it was directed by William Wellman, supposedly a man's man and an expert on regimental life. The unit apparently had to live in tents in the Mojave Desert – Lord knows why! Sternberg had proved in *Morocco* that sand was a studio property. Of course, what *Beau Geste* really lacks is anyone like Marlene Dietrich – but as you may have heard, such stuffed Englishmen as the Geste brothers actually believed in the Foreign Legion to escape the nerve-wracking fuss of women and because they had too much honour in their heads to leave room for sex. It's amazing that *Beau Geste* appeared just before the Second World War started – unless its inglorious assembly of lies, clichés and myths is the sort of thing

that makes real wars that much easier to get away
with.

Gary Cooper was close to his peak in 1939, and it's
worth remembering that he was taken very seriously by
David Selznick as a possibility for Rhett Butler in *Gone
With the Wind*. In hindsight, we all know that he was a
poor second to Clark Gable, and that's a way of saying
that Cooper lacked irony, or any kind of self-mockery.
The playfulness in *Gone With the Wind* is gone without
Gable – and Cooper, to give him his due, wanted nothing to do with it. Still, his way with clothes and drop-
dead repartee might have worked.

But Cooper was nearly as determined not to be in *The
Westerner* – and that turned out a sidelong jewel in that it
gave Coop the opportunity to study and overcome the
furiously wily Walter Brennan. For most Cooper enthu-
siasts, the contrast in that small Western between the
taciturn and the gabby is precious. But Cooper loathed
it as an assignment and came close to giving up on
Goldwyn in the process.

The story is very simple: a lone cowboy, Cole Harden,
drifts into the town ruled by Judge Roy Bean. Of course,
there was such a town in history – Langtry in Texas
(named after the Jersey Lily, Lillie Langtry, the sweet
apple of Bean's eye). This came from a novel by Stuart
Lake and a script by Niven Busch and Jo Swerling. This
was the picture where Cooper urged Busch to make
him the hero, and that was a sign of initial doubts over

The Westerner

Coop's participation in what was bound to end up a picture about Bean. That was Cooper's grievance on the project, and it was only accentuated when he saw how slowly and with what chewy delight Walter Brennan planned to eat his part. Not that Cooper's distress was directed at Brennan. The two actors were pals already and they bonded further over their shared dislike of Goldwyn. Brennan won the supporting actor Oscar as Bean. He commanded the picture, but that did not clash with the magical way in which the nearly meditative Cooper eventually killed the weasel chatterbox. The picture was a hit, and people came away from it relishing Cooper all the more.

His next assignment was as a Texas Ranger who pursues a target north of the border so that he meets up with the *North West Mounted Police*. It's a Cecil B. DeMille picture in which too much of the great outdoors is rebuilt on awkward sets where every footfall signals the wooden floor. And then comes *Meet John Doe*, one of the unyielding problem pictures of American film history. It was not nominated for Best Picture, or for Frank Capra's direction. It got a screenwriting nod, but Gary Cooper was passed over for acting. He had to be, I suppose, in that the same year he collected his inevitable Oscar for *Sergeant York*. We are coming to that bizarre film, so hard to stomach now, but as we do so, bear in mind that the alarming but arresting untidiness of *Meet John Doe* rests nearly entirely on the haggard, desperate look of Gary Cooper. It is as if he

Meet John Doe

smelled something in the air – decay or danger – that he
never dreamed was there before. And we can't get his
worry out of our heads. Alvin York is a hero bogus in
every detail, while Long John Willoughby is an authen-
tic American derelict. Cooper never did anything with
more subtlety.

Anne Mitchell (Barbara Stanwyck) is a writer on
the *Free Press*. But when the paper is bought out by
the *New Bulletin* a lot of worthy journalists are fired.
Anne is one of them, and no pleading can protect
her. So as a last column she pulls the old fakeroo: she
concocts a letter to the paper from 'John Doe', not
just out of work, but so alienated from the world and
its ways that he announces his own suicide on Christ-
mas Eve (Capra liked those big days the way Hitch-
cock revered American monuments). Of course,
there is no 'John Doe', just the men of America and
Anne's inventiveness. But a horde of real derelicts
come to the *Bulletin* looking for a handout – they are
the gaunt figures from Dorothea Lange – and one of
them is Coop: badly dressed, unwashed, with a bat-
tered fedora and a lick of hair on his brow. He could
be an outlaw; he could be Huck Finn grown old. He
looks melancholy and dangerous at the same time,
and his locked-in shyness is not far from violence.
With one look, I suggest, he makes Henry Fonda's
Tom Joad (from *The Grapes of Wrath*) seem like a figure from a Hallmark charity card.

His name is Long John Willoughby and he was a

baseball pitcher until his arm went dead. Even now, he seems to depend on 'the Colonel' (Walter Brennan), a catcher ally from those days. They play baseball without a ball. They do harmonica duets. And the Colonel is some kind of sane corrective to the madness that Long John seems to see waiting for him. It is a wry, tender friendship they have, and it is Brennan again, the best supporting actor Cooper ever found. (You can even imagine them, for a moment, like Lear and his Fool.) The film is a love story at heart – Coop and Stanwyck share the main credits title – but it's hard to believe this Coop can exist without the Colonel. Perhaps the idea of love is there to defeat the very scary warnings in the picture about an America of vagrants ready to form a 'John Doe Society' that might carry the wicked newspaper editor (Edward Arnold) to power.

The point is crucial: for this John Doe really is an outcast and not just an unlucky fellow who will be salved by having Anne as his soothing sweetheart. Of course, he becomes John Doe, and there is an uncanny radio broadcast where Cooper shifts from a guy who can hardly read his text (written by Anne) to a fired-up 100 per cent actor. Cooper never did anything more difficult or extended. He begins to believe in the fascism that lurks within her silly, sentimental view of John Doeism rescuing the world, and despite Capra's adroit use of the Colonel's weary disbelief to undercut every piece of humbug. But Willoughby knows he is the fakeroo, and even as he becomes smoother as Doe so

Cooper lets us see the cracks in the man's facade, the wounds left by lying.

What follows is more than problematic: it is a set-up in which Capra's pocket billiards version of politics drives Willoughby closer to real suicide. The makers of the film – Capra and scenarist Robert Riskin – had a terrible time working out how it should end – decently (or not). The picture has a happy ending, utterly unconvincing. It needed, I think, a fuller use of its own deepest virtue, of Willoughby being no longer fit for society or any amount of white lies. He might kill himself, or vanish. He could be as dangerous as Lonesome Rhodes (from Elia Kazan's *A Face in the Crowd* from 1957), and he could easily become the monster Anne has created. So the film is broken-backed (despite its nagging skills), but in Cooper's being it is a true glimpse into the turmoil of America in the '30s and the ease with which the clichés of ordinariness could turn to violence. 'Just make me the hero' bumps up against the dread in the actor's eyes – and it leaves scenes that are beyond Capra's film and the normal caution in being Gary Cooper. To see it is to long to remake it.

Whereas, it takes a dismayed historian's dedication to sit through *Sergeant York*, the alleged glory of Gary Cooper's career. This is the story, made on the eve of America entering the Second World War, about one of the great heroes from the First World War – Alvin York, the Tennessee farm boy, pious fundamentalist and self-trained sharpshooter, who would win the Congressional Medal of Honor despite his avowed feelings against war and such because of his religious devoutness. For York had gone to war under the label of 'conscientious objector' and with all the pacific attitudes of a reformed drunk and fighter. It is stomach-turning nonsense, despite the slavish care that director Howard Hawks takes over the humbug and despite Cooper's shameless imitation of a holy idiot persuaded to shoot down Germans as if they were a flight of wild duck.

Jesse Lasky, the mogul at Paramount once, had been trying to film the York story for twenty years, apparently unconcerned by the clash of martial patriotism and peaceful instincts. And as the new war approached so the mood turned in his favour. York – still alive – signed a deal for the film to be made, and Warner Brothers agreed to take it on. At the outset, it was hard for the people involved to imagine anyone but Gary Cooper in the lead role, so a deal was done with Goldwyn whereby Cooper and Bette Davis shifted camp for the one picture (she would do *The Little Foxes* and Cooper would play Alvin York). A script was done, by Abem Finkel and Harry Chandlee. It was only then that the project picked up Hawks as its director, as Hawks was fired by Howard Hughes from *The Outlaw*. Hawks was ready: Gary Cooper had been best man at the director's recent marriage to Nancy 'Slim' Gross. In later years, Hawks went so far as to float a story that he had persuaded Cooper to do the film as a favour to Lasky. But if anything, it's more likely that the actor persuaded the director. Cooper had been wary at first of playing a real hero. But he met York and bowed to the real man's encouragement. He studied Tennessee only to the extent that his own laconic delivery took on a rural twang and a lack of grammar. This is a way of regarding country life for people who have no intention of ever going to the country.

Hawks wanted a niftier script, and he brought Howard Koch and John Huston on board to supply it. The director was not himself a pursuer of country life, or a believer in rural talk and thinking. But Hawks had the commercial good sense to realize that this project was golden – so don't mess with. It was pro-war, while congratulating itself on vague pacific hopes; it was bloodthirsty and pious at the same time. But it was Gary Cooper who would do the most lying by lending his mighty 'sincerity' to the horribly patronizing view of Alvin York and the bamboozling of his rustic mind. And so the Tennessee naïf becomes a doughboy. Just like in the hill country, he wets the sight on his rifle to cut the haze and nails every target. There is a painful scene where he and a couple of officers swap Bible quotations before York sees that war and its ways are justified in the name of America and Daniel Booneism. Cooper signals every effect, and turns himself into an obedient parrot. The humiliation and manipulation of York is passed over. His extensive lack of intelligence bows to the film's greed for having and eating its cake at the same time. Fraud is not often a term one feels

As Sergeant York, with the good book

drawn to with Gary Cooper – if only because of the great care with which he hid behind barricades of sincerity. But this is a tricksy piece of work in which an actor's cunning assists in the brushing aside of a complex philosophy.

You can say it hardly mattered, that it was all in a noble cause and that Alvin York himself reckoned it was well done. All of which only indicates the film begging to be made about the hero as a confidence trickster. The picture reeks of sentimentality and deceit, yet it was nominated for eleven Oscars. In the category of Best Picture it was a loser (along with *The Maltese Falcon*, *The Little Foxes* and *Citizen Kane*) to *How Green Was My Valley*. But Gary Cooper won his first Oscar and beat out Orson Welles along the way. Much more than that, the picture earned over $6 million in rentals. That put it third, all-time, to *Gone With the Wind* and *Snow White*. It was enough to make Gary Cooper the country's number one box-office attraction. There are not many clearer examples in movie history of the conjunction of glory and barefaced theft.

But if you were to put certain moments of *Meet John Doe* and *Sergeant York* side-by-side on a screen, the smugness of the biopic, its self-satisfied drawling, would only guide you into the haunted alienation of Long John Willoughby. Compared with York, snug and pleased with himself in the army, Willoughby is from a hospital for the deranged, the forgotten man of 1930s folklore. Grasp that and suddenly Cooper's beauty becomes like a damaged sainthood – he is the social outcast who might become a helpless outlaw. Yet he is everyman, too. *Meet John Doe* is very carefully wrapped and ribboned at the end, but you know you're holding a bomb. You can feel its lively ticking. In comparison, *Sergeant York* is an overcooked turkey.

So now the Cooper machine was rolling. Every good project wanted him. The next in line was *Ball of Fire*, a far happier job for Howard Hawks. Sam Goldwyn was irritated that Cooper's films on loan-out were stronger commercially than anything the actor ever did for Uncle Sam. Somehow he thought of comedy. Paying over $80,000, he lured a hot writing team from Paramount – Billy Wilder and Charles Brackett – and encouraged them on an outline from their own files, about a linguistics professor and a burlesque dancer. They didn't fit, except they were crazy about each other – get it? And Goldwyn saw Coop as the tight-lipped, gently spoken language professor. It makes you suddenly fond of Goldwyn. How did Goldwyn lift Brackett and Wilder? He promised Paramount they could have Cooper for a thing called *For Whom the Bell Tolls*. You can see how easily a man like Cooper – homespun, straightforward – could reckon that in Hollywood you had your cake and you ate it, and then you took the next guy's piece.

You sometimes hear it said that *Ball of Fire* is not quite a masterpiece, and I daresay that in the company of films like *His Girl Friday* and *Bringing Up Baby*, that view is tenable. But then you have to come up with a standard for intense, renewable enjoyment, allied to the very profound chemical possibility – essentially American – that every girl ever called 'Sugarpuss' just needs an hour or two with a PhD (or a gang of them) to be worthy of the presidency. Just as no romance is more quickly stupefying than the 'made in heaven' kind, so none is likely to be longer lasting than the marriage of slap-bang opposites and a learned researcher's first exposure to thighs and stockings.

As the script unfolded (driven by a Wilder who was himself eager to direct), so Howard Hawks was sold as director to a begrudging Goldwyn. It is hard to credit now, but many actresses shied away from Sugarpuss, thinking the role might be a touch too vulgar. Ginger Rogers, Jean Arthur and Carole Lombard all said 'no', whereupon Coop himself – not long from the lingering and plainly infatuated glances of Barbara Stanwyck – suggested the casting we now regard as obvious. Do actors know best, or was Coop actually involved with Stanwyck? In the end, we have only the evidence on the screen to go by and the reports that Coop could hardly walk past a mare without a thought arising (in the mare's head). I think the principle of opposites had been at work.

Of course, Hawks moved in on the rest of the casting and saw that the whole picture was a version of a faculty vs kids ball game. So we have Oscar Homolka, Henry Travers, S. Z. Sakall, Tully Marshall, Leonid

Pottsy and Sugarpuss, *Ball of Fire*

Kinsky, Richard Haydn and Aubrey Mather as the other professors engaged on their dictionary, with Dana Andrews (Joe Lilac) and Dan Duryea (Duke Pastrami) as the two hoods who want to reclaim Sugarpuss O'Shea for the dowdy life of liquor and crime. I should have added that Coop's part is Bertram Potts, not just an adorable figure of tongue-tied shyness but a man Stanwyck can address as 'Pottsy'. Moreover, if only at the level of flirtatious device, Cooper seems happy and occupied with the recesses of appeal evident in a man whose spare time has hitherto been spent in intellectual pursuits. Just as in *Bringing Up Baby*, here is Hawks's wise advice that even book-writers must have a little fun now and then for the sake of their prose style. It is a proper moment to pause, I think.

Lou Gehrig had played in 2,130 games for the New York Yankees without a break. He was known as the 'Iron Man'. But he was not himself as the 1939 season started: he could not hit, he could not field. Then one day in the dressing room he fell over as he tried to put on his pants. His team-mates were aghast, and Gehrig took himself out of the line-up. In June, he went to the Mayo Clinic and it was from there that Dr Harold Habein issued this report: Lou Gehrig 'is suffering from amyotrophic lateral sclerosis. This type of illness involves the motor pathways and cells of the central nervous system.' It was, and still is, incurable – but now it is called Lou Gehrig's disease. On 4 July, the Yankees declared Lou Gehrig Appreciation Day. Gehrig then gave one of the most remembered speeches in American history. Despite a 'bad break', he let it be known that he regarded himself as 'the luckiest man on the face of the earth'. A little less than two years later he was dead.

Niven Busch, the Goldwyn story editor, proposed a movie about this hero. Goldwyn flinched: he knew little about baseball, and he reckoned that if people wanted to see the game they went to the park. So Busch showed his boss the newsreel of Gehrig's speech. That did it. The project was on and both men found that they were in unison on one thing: no one but Gary Cooper could be Lou Gehrig.

They would call it *The Pride of the Yankees* – to stress how much was at stake – and Paul Gallico was hired to write a suitably sentimental version of Gehrig's story. It was not hard: the player came from humble origins, but he had got himself through Columbia and – in the era of Babe Ruth – he was known (and rather despised by Ruth) as a clean-living fellow. Busch urged Gallico to underline the love story between Gehrig and his wife – in part because he needed to build up the female audience, but also because he hoped to marry Teresa Wright, the actress in line for Mrs Gehrig.

No matter the care that planned Cooper's life, he was horrified at being Lou Gehrig. He had not the least natural talent for baseball and he envisaged hours of grim practice trying to imitate the great man's swing and his stride. He was also intimidated by the idea of presenting himself as yet another lofty American hero. No argument mattered. Mrs Gehrig lent her support and talked to Cooper. He had a double for long-shots. He practised till he hated baseball. And for the crucial close-shots at the plate, to imitate Gehrig's left-handedness, the rightie Cooper wore a uniform with the 'Gehrig' printed backwards. When he swung at the plate, he ran towards third base and the film strip was then flip-flopped. The Tricks of the Yankees.

As to the natural humility of Gehrig, the athlete's modesty and the victim's pathos, Cooper was a natural for what is one of the classic male weepies and a preparation for war in which men might be moved by their own demise. Bit by bit, the inroads of sorrow and self-pity were settling into Gary Cooper's once dashing features.

The Pride of the Yankees was released on 5 March 1943. As an enshrinement of Gehrig's valour and a facsimile of his farewell speech it had had no equal in American history. The impact was aimed at the war, of course, but the confusion of historical event and dramatization was more lasting and more undermining. Cooper 'does' Gehrig with respect and fidelity, you may decide. But the mere reproduction of such an event speaks to a slowly escaping reality in American life. It was as if every real hero was now intent on getting an actor to 'be' him. The full damage to integrity has still not been measured. But the identification of Gary Cooper

As Lou Gehrig in *The Pride of the Yankees*

with an American ideal – the shy noble man under pressure – was established. Decades later, the country would ask itself whether the American flag had been raised over Iwo Jima (1945) in quite the movie-esque way depicted in photographs and memorials, but the substitution of Cooper's actorly eloquence for Gehrig's rather blank desperation goes uninspected.

The Pride of the Yankees earned rentals of over $4 million, and it was nominated for eight Oscars – including Best Picture, and for Wright and Cooper. He lost to James Cagney in *Yankee Doodle Dandy*.

Ernest Hemingway started to write *For Whom the Bell Tolls* in 1939. He worked in some sense of defeat after his own Spanish adventure and in the rueful, yet romantic mood of the end of his second marriage. The new novel took hold of him and became a tragedy about the lost republican cause in Spain, and the deep-felt love affair between Robert Jordan, an American fighting for the cause, and Maria, a Spanish girl who has been raped by the Fascists.

Jordan was a professor of literature at the University of Montana – the intellectual in the countryman – and he looked a lot like Coop: 'he was tall and thin, with sun-streaked fair hair, and a wind- and sun-burned face'. Hemingway had heard Marlene Dietrich talk about Cooper, but the author and the actor did not meet until soon after the novel was finished. They were together in the area of Sun Vally, Idaho, on shooting vacations.

Hemingway found that he was not nearly as well dressed as the cowboy. The actor was the better shot. But they got on, and Hemingway was heard to say that he believed Cooper was the actor to play Jordan if a film deal was ever worked out.

This came to pass even as the shooting holiday went on. Hemingway would get $150,000 for the movie rights (a record at that time). Then, a little later – as we have seen – Cooper was loaned away by Goldwyn to Paramount to play the hero. By then, the book was a best-seller. Hemingway and Cooper were of a mind that Howard Hawks was ideally suited to direct the film. But Paramount wouldn't listen. They assigned it to Sam Wood, instead, and they asked Dudley Nichols to do a script. Worst of all, seeing Maria as an exotic character, Paramount planned to cast the ballerina Vera Zorina, very striking looking, but possessed of a harsh voice and an unbending acting personality.

No one was more horrified at the Zorina casting than David O. Selznick, the man who had brought Ingrid Bergman to Hollywood, who had her under contract and was genuinely eager to please his emotional star. He had already loaned her out to Warners to play Ilsa in *Casablanca*, and he knew that Bergman longed to play Maria as much as Vivien Leigh had once been consumed with the role of Scarlett O'Hara. Hemingway himself had told the press that he thought Ingrid was right for Maria. Writer and actress met, in San Francisco, and the writer assured her she'd get the part.

But Paramount stayed out of the loop and the picture moved up to the Sierra foothills, with Zorina still in the lead. *Casablanca* was shot, and Ingrid feared she was looking too well to play the peasant girl Maria. But then rumours came down the mountains that Zorina was not quite cutting it, and was stepping from mountain rock to mountain ledge as daintily as Bambi if only not to risk damaging her legs. One day, while posing with Paul Henreid at Warners doing publicity shots for *Casablanca*, Ingrid got a call from Selznick and he told her she'd have to have her hair cropped short – she had the coveted part.

She got a train immediately to the location in Sonora and saw this 'beautiful man' coming down the slope. He called out to her 'Hallo, Maria?' Then a little later, he came up to her and he slipped into the dialogue from their film.

'I thought he was still talking to me,' Bergman would write later, because he didn't change his voice. He didn't become an actor who acted, he was exactly the same. So I kept saying, "Excuse me, what did you say? I can't understand what you're talking about." And he said a little reprovingly, "I'm reading the dialogue, that's the dialogue." So I blushed again.

'You see you worked with him and you had a feeling of doing so little. He didn't do anything. He had no expression in his face or his eyes saying these things. He just chuckled away, and talked quietly and I thought, this is not going to be any good at all. This is not going to work. Then we shot the scene and I still said to myself, he doesn't do anything. Then I saw the rushes, and there he was . . . The personality of this man was so enormous, so overpowering – and that expression in his eyes and his face, it was so delicate and so under-played. You just didn't notice it until you saw it on the screen. I thought he was marvelous; the most under-playing and most natural actor I ever worked with.'

It was not long before the dialogue coach, Ruth Rob-erts, was saying, 'Really, Ingrid, you must stop looking at him like that. You sit there just looking! I know you're supposed to be in love with him in the picture, but not too much in love with him!'

It was apparent to observers, and it was predicted by those who knew Ingrid Bergman. The Swedish actress was married with a young daughter, but she was reck-lessly promiscuous – with co-workers and with fascin-ating men (like the photographer Robert Capa). For his part, marriage may have made Cooper more cau-tious, but it hadn't stopped his taste for affairs. It was said that, rather than get involved with co-stars, he had location romances with minor figures. But it is likely that he had had a fling with Barbara Stanwyck, and now a major love affair set in with Ingrid Bergman. It was not in her nature to be discreet or hidden: indeed, as actress and person, Ingrid had an unstoppable confes-sional urge. And now, at his peak as a popular favourite, Cooper determined that if he offended his wife – so be it. If the people loved him, surely he could stand rebukes at home? It's easy to think of him as a womanizer (that type is provided for in our culture), but the type is the more shallow and the less appealing because he usually falls for mere sex. 'Make me the hero,' suggests something harder to deal with and potentially more tragic. Gary Cooper fell in love with the woman. And in the star-filled clear skies of the Sierra location at night, in a sleeping bag or a hotel suite, these giddy romantics became characters, so that their real lives had to totter along behind them.

The film hardly suffered if the co-stars had such chemistry. But was there always something overly romantic in Hemingway's concept? For the novel is a thwarted love story such as can turn into a bestseller. When *For Whom the Bell Tolls* was published, it received a lot of criticism from the left, especially on the grounds that it had missed the nature of both fascism and communism while settling for an idyllic Spanish hinterland where an American professor might go camping and find a warm nymph in his sleeping bag. Inevitably, the film stressed that escapism, and with the several Spanish roles being played by Russians and Greeks, no wonder exoticism played its part. It is too long (170 minutes on first release), and the direction is slack, but it is a classic star vehicle. It was nominated for Best Picture (losing to *Casablanca*), for Cooper, Bergman, Akim Tamiroff and Katina Paxinou (the only big winner). It had rentals well over $6 million, and it delivered a suitably tragic ending with Maria carried away screaming

Hemingway, Coop and Bergman during *For Whom the Bell Tolls*
(with Paul Shields looking on)

as the wounded Jordan and his machine gun face the approaching Fascists. Of course, by 1943, it was a lot easier for a movie to take that pose than it would have been in 1937 (when the action is set). *For Whom the Bell Tolls* makes an adventure out of the Spanish Civil War – but in that fatal respect it plays fair by the novel and Hemingway's dreamy identification with a figure like Coop. Robert Jordan was like Alvin York and Lou Gehrig – 'real' heroes for whom everyone could shed a tear. And it was Cooper's great good luck that his terse style coincided with America's attitude to the crisis it faced. He was a man fit for a boys' world.

As *For Whom the Bell Tolls* completed shooting, Gary Cooper was free of all attachments to studio contracts. But as the number one box-office draw (Bob Hope was the nearest to a rival), he elected to make his own way in the business. It was not so much that he had particular ambitions that gnawed at him. Instead, he sought to capitalize on his position and to escape the heavy income-tax charges. As a producer, he could file for a much lower tax rate. For the moment, all he did as a free man was to perpetuate his enslavement to Ingrid Bergman: he asked Warners to make something else – anything else – with the two of them. It proved to be *Saratoga Trunk*, from an Edna Ferber novel, with little other excuse than a chance to indulge the lead players. Sam Wood directed them again, and Casey Robinson wrote the script. Cooper was Colonel Clint Maroon and

Ingrid played Clio Dulaine – the romance was set in New Orleans. And the film ran badly over budget and schedule because the two leads were often late or unavailable. If only the film could have recorded what was delaying them.

For a moment, the great star thought of producing his own pictures – and it was not the worst idea in the world. *Along Came Jones* was meant to be a spoof on Westerns in which Gary played a singing cowboy (Melody Jones) who is mistaken for a mean killer (actually played by Dan Duryea). The picture was set up at Universal under Bill Goetz. Nunnally Johnson wrote it from an Alan Le May novel, and Stuart Heisler directed. Loretta Young was cast as the female lead. Coop did his best to act like a producer and he got a reputation for being a skinflint when he made Ms Young's clothes cheaper. But the script is what needed work, just as the whole movie was woefully short of wit.

And so the slippage set in. *The Story of Dr. Wassell* was one of the limpest films Cecil B. DeMille would ever make. It's another real-life hero from the recent war, Corydon Wassell, a doctor who stayed with wounded American soldiers on Java and took them all the way to safety. The budget was $2.7 million (with Cooper on $200,000). There was arduous jungle shooting. And Wassell was another religious man, temperamentally shrinking from violence and kissing the girl (Laraine Day). Screenwriter Charles Bennett was rebuked by DeMille for writing lines too elegant for Cooper. 'He

wasn't a great actor,' said Bennett. 'He was a personality.' The film opened in July 1944 – after D-Day – and
by then the audience wanted a more confident and
aggressive type of heroism.

The one picture of this period that held promise was
Cloak and Dagger. Milton Sperling had persuaded Warners to make a really topical film – something about the
technological developments and the attendant espio-
nage that became so notable at the end of the war.
Several writers had tried it without success. But then,
at about the same time, Fritz Lang came in to direct,
Gary Cooper agreed to play the lead role – Dr Alvah
Jasper – and Ring Lardner Jr was hired to work on the
script. When Lardner and Cooper met, the worried
actor told the writer: 'Look, I want you to understand
one thing. I'm supposed to be playing an atomic physicist in this picture. And the only way I can get away with
playing an atomic physicist is if you keep the lines very
simple, because I can't be convincing as an atomic
physicist if I try to say anything complicated.'

Still, Cooper was getting $500,000 to be a cross
between Oppenheimer and James Bond. It's an adventure film, with a good deal of violence, but it is shot
through with intimations of a brave, if fearful, new
world. There was even an ending intended, at a deserted
Nazi research centre under the mountains, a place where
60,000 slave labourers are found slaughtered, where Jasper was to say that this was a new dawn in which America had the responsibility of handling nuclear power.

Alas, that is missing and so an important picture remains an excellent piece of routine work

The female lead was a very young Lilli Palmer, and you can feel that she and Coop have a real interest in each other. But Lang treated Palmer very badly during the shooting. So it was characteristic of the star to approach her afterwards and mumble: 'Hey, kid, say, that business with Lang, you know – I probably should have . . . uh, but you see, I'm . . . not much good at that sort of thing. I never seem to find the right words. I need a script. Know what I mean?'

In the years just after the war, there were several outstanding American pictures, with performances to match – Fredric March in *The Best Years of Our Lives*, Jimmy Stewart in *It's a Wonderful Life*, Roberts Ryan and Mitchum in *Crossfire*, Bogart and Walter Huston in *The Treasure of the Sierra Madre*, Broderick Crawford in *All the King's Men*, Gregory Peck in *Twelve O'Clock High*, Ray Milland in *The Lost Weekend*. How many of those parts could Cooper have played? Or was it that he was too settled, or not discerning enough to see the cracks appearing in the American bowl? Could he have done the alcoholic in *The Lost Weekend*? Or Peck's officer on the way to a nervous breakdown in *Twelve O'Clock High*?

These are questions worth answering if one feels dumbfounded by what he did: a flat version of Hawkeye fighting Indians and the white men who mislead them in DeMille's *Unconquered*, and the nice guy in Leo McCarey's *Good Sam*. These are not good enough pictures for a top star, and they are unchallenging in a moment of great change. So maybe Cooper was too narrowly heroic? But then recall that in the same years John Wayne broke his own fixed pattern with Tom Dunson in *Red River* and Sergeant Stryker in *The Sands of Iwo Jima*. One may love Coop, but I don't think he would have played Dunson better than Wayne did.

But then in one film everything changed.

Ayn Rand's *The Fountainhead* was published in 1943, ignoring the war, and insisting on the proper selfishness that drove people of genius – like Howard Roark the architect. It's easier now than it was then to see how accurately Ms Rand had identified a modern subject: the need for dramatic vision in great public buildings, and the way in which that vision must stay private, inspired and uncompromised by urban manoeuvring. In 1943, the world – more or less – was knocking buildings down and all pulling together. Today, we believe in buildings as our shared art, rather in the way film was in the war years.

So *The Fountainhead* was and remains a powerful film, just as millions of young people come to Ayn Rand as new readers every year. Howard Roark is based loosely on Frank Lloyd Wright (in his battles with clients, critics and society), but Roark is also the articulate mouthpiece of Rand's hot gospel. He is physically impressive (he is a construction, if you like), but he has to talk, too, and how does a genius talk when he's played by Gary Cooper?

It was not always Cooper as Roark. At Warners, where the film was made, Humphrey Bogart got a lot of consideration. He had a harsh, cold side; you could credit his inner intelligence; and he could carry dialogue with wit and a nearly pugilistic force. But Bogie was a small man, and if you asked him to hold a rock drill and look as if he understood the symbolism he was most likely to give you a sour grin. Gary Cooper seldom stooped to noticing symbols, so he could pick up a rock drill and it was a part of him – at least, that's how it seemed on the face of Patricia Neal, the actress who would be watching him.

Her role was Dominique Francon, the beautiful young mistress to media tycoon Gail Wynand (Raymond Massey), the woman who starts by opposing Roark and then becomes his accomplice in everything he does. Barbara Stanwyck had read the book early and felt the part belonged to her. She had told Warners about it, but later on they would claim that they had known already. Bette Davis may have been considered, as well as Ida Lupino and Eleanor Parker. But the part went to Patricia Neal, a beautiful blonde from Packard, Kentucky, and Northwestern, who was twenty-five years younger than Cooper. They fell madly in love – indeed, I think it was the biggest love of Cooper's life, and it came to him at a point of vulnerability where he was starting to feel his age.

The Fountainhead probably bewildered many Cooper fans. The film received no Academy Award nominations, and not too many strong reviews. It was always going to be an Ayn Rand film, even if the writer had not done her own own screenplay and urged the casting of Cooper instead of Bogart. As directed by King Vidor, it is sometimes a breathless study in camp energies, with visual symbols and talk perched on the edge of plausibility as populism struggles with elitism. It is a mess, but a very American mess, and one that has not come close to dying yet, in the way *Unconquered* and *Good Sam* have been put to rest. *The Fountainhead* is compulsive and unforgettable. It is a dream – if you like – or a rapture, a vein of romanticism to which Gary Cooper very seldom committed himself. Yet there is no shirking or shyness here, and perhaps it is because Patricia Neal has led him on. Their chemistry is not just capital 'C' – it deserves a 'K'. This is one of the very few American films that really inhabits the life of the mind, in which an architect is also a bomber who destroys buildings, a genius and a demon and close to a rapist. It is probably the most extraordinary acting Gary Cooper ever turned in – and it is possible that he was changed and moved by it. Why should actors not respond to their overheated material if we are meant to?

They fell in love, Neal and Cooper, as the filming went on, though they claimed that they never made love until the shooting was over. Such professionalism hardly matters. On screen, the woman's utter need for this natural master is delivered with reckless force – I mean by that that it's a close call whether the audience

With Patricia Neal in *The Fountainhead*

laughs or goes with the heady romance. Neal was intelligent: I think she had a better mind than Cooper had ever dreamed of. And it's likely that her understanding of their characters was a spark for their own love. Though close to fifty, Cooper is a splendid figure throughout the film, his face full of Roark's certainty. And in real life, Coop was flying. He had just made a new and lucrative deal with Warners (*The Fountainhead* was its opening picture). He had lately built a new house in Aspen, Colorado, and instead of it being a family place it became his love nest with Neal. And so it happened that the lifelong philanderer and natural coward decided that his marriage was over. He and Rocky separated for a period of years. Coop and Neal were a press item and from time to time they believed they would be married. As never before, he seemed able to test how well he could think of himself. Almost immediately, ageing set in. If that seems too neat, look at the photographs from these years yourself. I think they leave no doubt about the complexity of the crisis Cooper had created for himself.

Many passages from *The Fountainhead*, and the muddle of Cooper's private life, suggested how ready he was for challenging roles. And one suspects that really big pictures with dangerous themes might have carried Cooper and Neal into marriage. As it is, it's clear that his doubts or timidity only grew. Rocky was an intimidating force (some onlookers felt she bullied him) and she used her Catholic faith as a lever with him. Maria, their daughter, was in her early teens. And Cooper had a great need to be respectable or admirable, even if he sounded like an idiot in the process.

Such a case had occurred in 1947. It was in that year that the House Committee on Un-American Activities made its first serious assault on 'leftists' in Hollywood. In October, under the chairmanship of J. Parnell Thomas, the Committee first called a number of 'friendly' witnesses to Washington to testify to the gravity of the problem. These witnesses included Louis B. Mayer, Adolphe Menjou, Robert Taylor, director Sam Wood and Gary Cooper. The Committee was trying to convey the suggestion – ludicrous to many people – that the American movie was infiltrated with Red ideas. Cooper was not a relaxed witness – after all, he had no script (or was there one?), and he was a good deal more hesitant than Longfellow Deeds. But he could not help but remind viewers of that ideal American.

So Coop said that he had heard people question the Constitution – a thing allowed for in that very document. When asked if he had ever been offered scripts that had communistic suggestions (like *Cloak and Dagger*, *Meet John Doe* or *For Whom the Bell Tolls*?), Cooper reckoned he had. What were their titles? the question came back. But the actor couldn't remember. He was feeble at best, ridiculous at worst, but he agreed with Thomas that the Communist Party in America should be outlawed: 'I think it would be a good idea, although

I have never read Karl Marx and I don't know the basis of communism, beyond what I have picked up from hearsay. From what I hear, I don't like it because it isn't on the level.' This is mealy-mouthed humbug, of course, but Coop had spent his life uttering such lines so that Americans nodded and took the drivel to heart.

Alas, the films that followed *The Fountainhead* certainly were free from Red ideas, but only because it was hard for anyone to see any of them sustaining any ideas.

It's a Great Feeling was a Warner Brothers collective in which Jack Carson and Dennis Morgan made fun of Hollywood. Cooper was one of many studio stars to make a cameo appearance.

In *Task Force*, directed by Delmer Daves, Cooper played a naval officer who believes in aircraft carriers. Jane Wyatt was his co-star.

Bright Leaf (directed by Michael Curtiz) had Cooper as a pioneer figure in the tobacco industry and two women in his life (Lauren Bacall and Patricia Neal). The most interesting thing about the picture is that one female role was much more exciting than the other. Guess who got it? No, Bacall won the part, simply because Cooper – who was known as Neal's lover at the time – could not muster the energy to speak up on her behalf. In its way, that story goes deeper into the haplessness of Gary Cooper than anything I can offer. It was also one incident among many that served as the writing on the wall for Neal.

And yet, at the same time, Cooper would accompany

Pat Neal to acting classes given by Jeff Corey – who had a famous school in Hollywood, and who was well known as being a political radical. Corey recalled a class where he really engaged Cooper with analysis, yet the star admitted he was stale – he had been away on a safari with Hemingway. 'Oh, I really enjoyed working on the scene with you,' he told Corey. 'I have only one or two tricks at best.' Corey was amazed and he tried to convince Cooper how far his naturalness had guided a generation of actors. Cooper was intrigued by the classes, but he could never bring himself to criticize another actor.

Dallas: a routine Western, directed by Stuart Heisler, wth Ruth Roman in the lead.

You're in the Navy Now: a naval comedy set against the war. A disaster.

It's a Big Country: mindless patriotism, and another cameo role.

Distant Drums: a halfway decent Western, written by Niven Busch and directed by Raoul Walsh, set in the Florida Everglades, with Mari Aldon as the female lead – and the beneficiary of an affair with Cooper (his first infidelity with Patricia Neal).

That run of seven films is the drabbest in Cooper's career. It began to open up a large rift between what he was earning and what his pictures were worth, and it seemed to confound the possibility that he was aroused or stimulated by being with Patricia Neal.

*   *   *

And so we come to *High Noon*.

It was a script by Carl Foreman, and the last real work he delivered before being blacklisted (he had refused to confirm or deny Communist Party membership in further HUAC hearings). The producer Stanley Kramer saw it as a modestly budgeted film ($750,000) and he persuaded Fred Zinnemann to direct it for just $60,000 up front plus points off the gross. It seems clear that Zinnemann and Kramer saw Gary Cooper in the lead, but they were worried about his slipping stature and did consider Brando or Clift. Then they managed to convince Coop to do the film on the same terms as Zinnemann enjoyed.

Of course, Cooper's age raised certain problems in the script: for the action occurs on Cooper's wedding day to a much younger Quaker woman. It is also apparent that the sheriff – Will Kane – has a Mexican woman (Katy Jurado) in town with whom he has been involved. This can be only a guess, since no one has owned up to it, but I suspect Foreman and Zinnemann kept this rather odd sexual/romantic background in place if only because they knew how confused Cooper's own life was at the time. In a way, Kelly's part might seem to be a metaphor for Patricia Neal. But Neal never looked kindly upon that reading after she learned how – up in Sonora, on location – Coop had been fucking Grace Kelly. (Or was it the other way round? It may be easier to see her as the active force.)

Zinnemann was only aware of how far Cooper's

developing arthritis tested him for the role – with fist-fights, many walking scenes and the final shoot-out. More than ever before, in *High Noon* Cooper's walk is guarded or cautious, and the pain on his face is never quite wiped away.

In the years since, there have been arguments about what *High Noon* means – whether it is a tribute to the law-making resolve or a fable about a broken community. Yet it seems to me that it is about 84 expertly taut minutes. It is an action suspense film made without flaw or diversion. Floyd Crosby's photography, Zinnemann's direction and the great score by Dimitri Tiomkin (with the song 'Do Not Forsake Me, Oh My Darling', sung by Tex Ritter) all contribute towards a perfect but shallow work. The script is cut to the last inch and the supporting cast is excellent in what is so modest a film. The film ends in triumph, and it could have come out tragically. Either ending would work. And all of a sudden there is Gary Cooper fulfilled by his old, quaint hope. He is the hero. Maybe the last unequivocal hero in American film – at least until *Rocky*. *High Noon* grossed $18 million worldwide.

At the Oscars, it was nominated for Best Picture and lost to *The Greatest Show on Earth*. Zinnemann was nominated but he lost to John Ford for *The Quiet Man*. But Gary Cooper won his second Oscar, defeating Brando in *Viva Zapata*, Kirk Douglas in *The Bad and the Beautiful*, José Ferrer in *Moulin Rouge*, and Alec Guinness in *The Lavender Hill Mob*. The score and the song won, too.

High Noon

Carl Foreman was soon forced to leave America to find work, but Gary Cooper walking the deserted streets of his small town became one of the great ambivalent images in American film. We are left to wonder at the honeymoon Sheriff Kane will enjoy with his Quaker wife.

In 1952, the Coopers were reconciled. Not long thereafter Patricia Neal married Roald Dahl, the writer. The serene press pictures of Cooper's private life resumed, but in truth nothing was ever the same again. He was always looking for love affairs, and that reputation began to cloud over his noble image. As the '50s advanced, Cooper's reputation grew more interesting and poignant as he had a succession of flawed characters to play.

Springfield Rifle was a conventional Western – with Phyllis Thaxter as the heroine and David Brian as the villain (B movie players) – but Cooper's character undergoes a false court-martial: he lives under the burden of his humiliation.

In *Return to Paradise*, Cooper was a beachbum in the South Pacific. Roberta Haynes played an island native girl and Cooper apparently told her that he would have pursued her but for the deflating influence of medication he was taking for ulcers. The dream was creaking in its joints.

On *Blowing Wild* – a reunion with Barbara Stanwyck and Anthony Quinn – set in the oilfields of Mexico, Cooper was observed being intimate with Stanwyck off-screen even if not that much happened on screen.

For *Vera Cruz*, the up-and-coming Burt Lancaster used his own production company (Hecht-Hill-Lancaster) to challenge Gary Cooper to a duel. Some friends warned Coop that Burt's energy would sweep him away. So Coop made the deal first: he would require $500,000 up front and 10 per cent of the gross. The cynical Western, directed by Robert Aldrich, proved a hit, and Coop's character finally killed Burt. But Cooper walked away with about $1.4 million (about twice the budget on *High Noon*).

Garden of Evil was the same kind of thing: three unsound men (Coop, Richard Widmark and Cameron Mitchell) are hired by Susan Hayward to find her lost husband and the chance of treasure. It was filmed on remote Mexican locations where Coop slept with a local woman and worked up a nice sarcastic on-screen bond with Widmark.

Then he was back in uniform for Otto Preminger's *The Court-Martial of Billy Mitchell*, the story of the officer who got himself into bad trouble by saying the navy was smothering the air force. Mitchell actually predicted Pearl Harbor, fifteen years early. It's not a great film, but Coop's anguish as a career officer who is ruined is heavily underlined by the court scenes where Cooper's stalwart underplaying is devoured by the excesses of Rod Steiger as the prosecuting officer.

Despite Oscar nominations (Best Picture, for director William Wyler, for supporting actor Anthony Perkins and for Michael Wilson's screenplay), *Friendly*

Persuasion is one of the dreariest films Cooper ever made. From a novel by Jessamyn West, it is a set of pieties about how a Quaker farmer handles the American Civil War. It's the kind of picture that gets respectability and serious themes a crushing reputation – worse, it is one in which people call each other 'thee' and 'thou'. But it was such a prestige picture it was nearly Cooper and Katharine Hepburn (Dorothy McGuire filled in). It made a lot of money and it won the Palme d'Or at Cannes. As far as one can tell, Cooper himself responded to the solemnity of the picture by having an affair with Anita Ekberg – the statuesque Swedish star. I know, it's late in the day for taste in these matters, but whereas it's possible to see and sympathize with a fling between Coop and Grace Kelly, Coop and Ekberg goes beyond our limits. It's as if a ladies' man for the ages has somehow given up the ghost. It's also a measure of the apparent silence that now existed between Cooper and his wife.

In his next film, the fifty-five-year-old would play with Audrey Hepburn.

Love in the Afternoon was aimed originally at Cary Grant or Yul Brynner. That's what Billy Wilder said, after he had had his first job with a new writing partner, I. A. L. Diamond. I'm sure it was so, but I think once it was clear that Gary Cooper would play Frank Flannagan, the roving American lothario, the writing slipped in a few notes from home – thus, among Flannagan's many past affairs, we hear about the twin sisters from Stock-holm, a Wilderian nod to the scarcely credible *poitrine* of the great Ekberg (only a ninth of which ever shows above water). So, at last, Gary Cooper found himself presented with a part of quiet but inescapable personal resonance. Make me a hero has changed to make me a man who travels the world and can't keep his hands off the attractive women he meets. Nothing in the film bothers to explain why. Flannagan is given no wife any-where who misunderstands him. Instead, the film is filled with understanding: he loves women, and a life where he can try to touch them all. It is his way of being alive and it might look ugly but for Cooper's grace.

Love in the Afternoon may also refer to Hemingway's *Death in the Afternoon*, for there is a gentle underscoring here that this promiscuity is close to death or a way of holding off that final partner. It derives from a Paul Czinner film of 1931, *Ariane*, and that is the name given to the daughter of the private detective (played respec-tively by Audrey Hepburn and Maurice Chevalier). It's when the father has to investigate the roué for a divorce case that Ariane gets to hear about him – she is Audrey Hepburn as cello-player, the eternal wise virgin, but her casting is so clear that she helps us see that while Coo-per as Flannagan is lined, weary, shot in shadow, and nearly broken by his own compromises, still he has an innocence to match hers. So the film's ending, with a totally movie-made gesture, is a way of saying that innocents can fall in love, no matter how far apart.

Did Cooper know that Wilder was making a movie about him? Well, on the one hand, if you see the movie now, it's hard to think anyone was missing the point. But Gary Cooper has few credentials when it comes to insight. He told some reporters on set that as he got to play men closer to his age so it got to be more realistic. But *Love in the Afternoon* is a fantasy, a very deliberate return to the style and vision of Lubitsch. It's a Paris of romantic possibility where a small band of gypsy musicians keep company with Flannagan – because there is always music playing when great stars hold the screen.

Cooper does not appear properly until twenty-five minutes into the picture (too long at two hours). He is kindly veiled in shadow and soft focus. He doesn't have too much to do except behave like an elderly God on earth. Hepburn has much more of the real acting to do – and far more of Wilder's attention and trust. And when, finally, instead of just admitting that these two are not real prospects for life, so their film asserts that they are dream figures who can only exist together.

Love in the Afternoon isn't perfect – and it might have been with Grant, who seemed to understand his own rake image so much better than Cooper and to feel sadness or disdain over it. But it is a touching farewell in the actor's career and an alternative to some mercilessly stupid films that seemed to satisfy him. So Cooper may not have understood the odd, delicate picture, and he certainly didn't have it in him to put the project together. But if you want to see why, even with his follies, Gary Cooper was still adored, this is the film.

His next picture again followed the storyline of a much older man and a younger woman. There was an epidemic of such films in the late '50s as several male stars hit middle age but preferred to be seen on screen (and in life, too, very often) with daughter figures. The pattern covered Gable, Fred Astaire, Bogart, John Wayne, Grant and Jimmy Stewart, but it felt most pronounced with Cooper. In *Ten North Frederick* he was Joe Chapin, a politician who falls in love with a friend of his daughter (Suzy Parker). It came from a John O'Hara novel, with a script by Philip Dunne who also directed. Diane Varsi played Chapin's daughter and Geraldine Fitzgerald was his hostile wife – a role Cooper knew from life. Ms Parker, once a model, was only twenty-five, yet she had been a close friend to Cooper's father-in-law, Paul Shields. Sometimes real life can make the age differences on screen seem small. *Ten North Frederick* didn't do very well, but it's an intriguing picture in which we see an unusually open and vulnerable Cooper.

Immediately thereafter, in sunshine and colour that served to expose his age and approaching illness, Gary Cooper made *Man of the West*. Far more clearly than *Love in the Afternoon*, this is a radical and quite brutal reappraisal of a lifetime in the screen's saddle, as well as a film that lives up to its epic title. Again, the question has to be asked – was Cooper himself aware of the way the picture summed up so much of his career and left his courage and energy stranded? Did he even consider that, in time, it might come to stand as a far more complex work than *High Noon*? Did he know how little time was left?

The screenplay was by Reginald Rose and the direction was by Anthony Mann, who had made a string of Westerns through the 1950s in which James Stewart played a man with a past who has to face that burden: *Winchester 73*, *Bend of the River*, *The Naked Spur*, *The Far Country*, *The Man from Laramie*. These are essential Westerns, and the bond between Mann and Stewart seemed strong. But a few years after the series, here was Mann with a story that needed Cooper's gravitas and his readiness for tragedy. It's obvious enough that Stewart could have played the part – but not with Cooper's pain or melancholy.

As the film begins we are in a small town in the West. Gary Cooper (Link Jones) comes riding in from out of the wilderness, with a mission. He seems to be a rural fellow, taken aback by city ways. He gets on the train that will go to Fort Worth (in Texas). Jones has a simple mission, though one seldom employed in the classic Western. He has the money to hire a schoolteacher who will travel out to the small community where Link lives, with his wife and children. The schoolteacher is quite plainly not the woman, Billie Ellis (Julie London), who is also on the train as a prostitute ordered out of town. But she and Link notice each other.

Along the way, the train is held up and everyone is

robbed. Link loses the money that is meant for a schoolteacher. Horses are taken, too, so Cooper, London and
another character (Arthur O'Connell) try to walk towards safety. In fact, Link leads them, for he has recognized some of the robbers. He takes them through soft,
green and mauve country, nothing like the place where
they were robbed. He is making not just a physical journey but a trip into his past.

And so he leads them to an isolated house, the place
where the Tobin gang hides away. The leader is Dock
Tobin (Lee J. Cobb), a mad father-figure, and the other
gang members are Jack Lord, Royal Dano, John Dehner
and Robert Wilke (a fair cross-section of the unwashed
dangerous men in '50s Westerns). Dock greets Link
with sour satisfaction – for Link was once part of the
Tobin gang, and a prized son-like figure for Dock.
Meanwhile, the gang members begin to make advances
on Billie Ellis. There is even a moment when, threaten-
ing Link's life, the gang compel Billie to take off her
clothes – or as many of them as censorship in the 1950s
would allow. Later on, in revenge, Link will strip the
Jack Lord character of his clothing. These sexual scenes
are very uneasy and they hint at the barely restrained
urge for rape in the Old West.

Link is hanging around for the schoolteacher money.
And so he pretends to go along with the Tobins in what
will be their last raid – a bank hold-up in a nearby town.
But 'nearby' hardly allows the violent shift from rural
setting to desert ghost town. The whole Tobin enter-

prise is revealed as insanity because there is no longer an active bank in the abandoned town. But there is a savage finale in which Link kills the several gang members, including Dock, but only after Dock has raped Billie Ellis. Link and Billie make their way back to the railhead. There will be a schoolteacher, but can he or she tame the last astonishing violence that helped bring the job into being?

Man of the West has flaws. Julie London is too lovely yet too inert for her role. Link's character might suffer a little more sexual confusion. No matter, this is a bleak version of the Western myth of how civilization developed, and of how narrowly the new integrity of the old outlaw made the journey. Far more than the earlier Cooper Westerns, it is an exploration of mythology and truth. So it is very helpful that we never see Link's community or his wife. Maybe they are sweet angels, all of them, but maybe they have their own ghosts to put to rest. What a film it would be if the wife turned out to be someone from the wrong side of respectability, like Billie. But that would reorder the plot. It needs a new film. As it is, every suggestion is in place; the man of the West came out of the swamp. And Cooper's presence sustains the film. He looks older than his age, more fragile (though there are desperate fights) and with very few resources left. The hero is not far from a scarecrow, and the acting is streets ahead of the self-satisfied impersonation of Alvin York.

* * *

Throughout the 1950s, Cooper had many operations
for hernias and ulcers. They bespeak a worrier who had
strained himself too often. But it was lung cancer that
was waiting, surely the consequence of so much casual
smoking.

There were four more films to go: *The Hanging Tree*
was a Western by Delmer Daves. Coop plays a doctor
with a bad past who nurses Maria Schell in blindness,
with Karl Malden and George C. Scott (in his debut)
as menacing presences. In Robert Rossen's *They Came
to Cordura*, Cooper is an officer – once charged with
cowardice – who has to guide a group of men across a
desert. It is a self-conscious parable, but it required a
strenuous physical commitment from Coop that is
often painful to watch. In *The Wreck of the Mary Deare*,
Cooper is a sea skipper charged with negligence and out
to prove himself. And in *The Naked Edge*, made in England, Deborah Kerr has to wonder whether her husband is a murderer.

It was not a good way to go, yet Cooper elected to
stay in work and to amass more money. He did not have
any more than he had ever had the drive or the execu-
tive ability to set up a picture for himself. But there was
one at least that he dreamed of: ever since the publica-
tion of Hemingway's *Across the River and into the Trees*
(1950), he had wanted to play Colonel Cantwell in a film
from it. It is a short novel on the last days of a tough
American officer who recalls the wars in northern Italy
as he has his last romance with a young Italian woman.

It has never been filmed, despite interest from many actors, and it is a book in which nothing much more happens than love and death. You could fill it out with flashbacks to the war, but I fear that would kill its voice. It's not too hard to think of Cooper, in the '50s, trying it, with Pier Angeli, with someone like Hawks directing. But it never came to pass.

So Cooper fought the long campaign with cancer, entered the Catholic Church, and was to all apparent signs a dutiful husband at last. Very few people knew the grim truth. But word reached the Academy, and in the ceremonies that occurred on 17 April 1961, an honorary Oscar was given to Coop. It was William Wyler who made the presentation and James Stewart who received it. He said he was sorry that Coop could not be there in person. The award was for 'his many memorable screen performances and the international recognition he, as an individual, has gained for the motion picture industry'. Stewart went on, 'We're very very proud of you Coop, all of us.' Then he broke down as he finished the speech, and suddenly the world realized that Cooper must be very close to death. Less than a month later he was gone. It is said that Ernest Hemingway watched the Oscars telecast and turned away, too moved to speak about the news. He was in his own last season. Cooper received cables from Jack Kennedy, the Queen of England and Alvin York, who lived until 1964.

Hemingway said several times that you had to be a

good man before you could be a good writer. It was wishful thinking, of course. We know in our hearts that there are great artists who must have been poisonous in life. Just as there are noble men who will put you to sleep. So, in a way, Hemingway had no business daydreaming over Gary Cooper. As early as 1932, the author had seen Cooper's *A Farewell to Arms* and known that the result was ridiculous. *For Whom the Bell Tolls* had been a much happier business, all round, but it was written in the spirit of a big movie – it deserved Ingrid and Coop. Equally, in any film of *Across the River and into the Trees*, the actor would have laboured with Papa's sententious dialogue – the kind of talk that came into a writer's head when he had been thinking he was Gary Cooper too much.

Gary Cooper was not the brightest soul, not the most intelligent or steadfast man. He could be weak, timid, self-indulgent, a snob, lazy, indifferent, an opportunist. None of which ever stopped him looking like Gary Cooper. And for as long as he had that facility – which is to say, to the end – he could set a famous author spinning as easily as this or that girl. Was he therefore a manipulator? I think not, because I fear he lacked the decisive intelligence, the cunning, to be so masterful. Late in life, on *The Wreck of the Mary Deare*, Charlton Heston met Cooper and was amazed at how easy it was to like the man. They were in the same hotel, and Coop would tell stories about the old days without boasting. When they went to rushes together, Heston found he couldn't take his eyes off Cooper.

Put Coop in a picture, let the light fall, and make him the hero – no, it wasn't that simple. There are hours of mediocre movies on the record and only a few Gary Cooper pictures of the first order – *Morocco, Desire, Mr. Deeds Goes to Town, Meet John Doe, Ball of Fire, The Fountainhead, High Noon, Man of the West*. That's only eight. Are there others that really ought to be in the first rank? Well, I'm not too sure that there are others, and once again I think that short supply needs to be taken as part of the Cooper story. Actors are what they do, and what they choose to do – especially actors with Cooper's power. In the early '40s he had as successful a run of pictures as anyone ever had, and he turned it to very little useful result.

On the other hand, he made a string of middling pictures in which he is loved – everything from *The Plainsman* to *The Westerner*, or from *Beau Geste* to *Lives of a Bengal Lancer*. I think it's a scandal that he wasn't allowed to do more comedy – for he had it in him to find comic timing of an unusual order. But he must take some of the blame for that and he, undoubtedly, fancied himself in heroic vein, or as someone a boy might admire.

I saw *High Noon* when I was ten – the perfect age. In this, I realize now, I was urged on by my father who plainly loved Cooper and based that affection on films like *Beau Geste, The Plainsman* and *The Lives of a Bengal Lancer*. So my dad told me in advance that *High Noon* was going to be terrific. And I had no power to resist or disagree. When I was ten it was a great film, one of my favourites and one that I saw several times. That means that Coop helped define courage for me as the sheriff who would rather stay and fight his deadly enemies instead of being off on honeymoon. At ten, I didn't think too much about that idyll, and didn't weigh the anxious townsmen who would not help their sheriff. I saw just his destiny – the necessary ordeal, the one he would not back away from for the sake of honour.

In time, I saw through *High Noon*. Hawks' *Rio Bravo* was meant as a critique of the earlier film and it argues the obvious case: that in a crisis you want people you can rely on, not stupid townspeople. But Carl Foreman, the writer, was onto something, too – something that might have horrified the conservative Cooper if he'd thought of it: that the town has become complacent and selfish and lazy after its frontier ordeal. It no longer sees that it needs to stand beside a sheriff. That is worthwhile, too. *High Noon*, among many other things, is the forlorn state of a chronic hero in a land that no longer keeps faith with his honour.

The real Gary Cooper? Well, I think he was a fool for a good suit and a willing woman, and bedding Grace Kelly up in Sonora is one thing, but falling for Anita Ekberg is another. It's a sign of the comic buffoon who didn't show his face too often. But if in the last resort Gary Cooper was a feeble family man, an adulterer and a betrayer, he was like many other people in the age of movies – he was romancing in his dreams. It was just that he was in an unusual position – in the saddle, as it were – and able to take advantage of it. Make me the hero, he said, and left us to wonder whether the line carried any irony.

A Note on Sources

A deeply revealing biography of Cooper remains to be written, but by far the best standard biography is Jeffrey Meyers' *Gary Cooper: American Hero* (New York, Harper-Collins, 1998). Other books that need to be read are Patricia Neal, *As I Am* (New York, Simon & Schuster, 1988); Hector Arce, *Gary Cooper: An Intimate Biography* (New York, William Morrow, 1979); and Stuart Kaminsky, *Coop: The Life and Legend of Gary Cooper* (New York, St Martin's Press, 1980).

Filmography

1923 *The Last Hour* (uncredited and unconfirmed)
1925 *Dick Turpin* (uncredited)
   The Trail Rider (uncredited)
   In the Days of the Thundering Herd (uncredited)
   Riders of the Purple Sage (uncredited)
   The Drug Store Cowboy (uncredited)
   Wild Horse Mesa (uncredited)
   The Lucky Horseshoe (uncredited)
   The Vanishing American (uncredited)
   The Eagle (uncredited)
   Tricks (uncredited)
   Warrior Gap (uncredited)
   North Star (uncredited)
   Ben-Hur: A Tale of the Christ (uncredited)
1926 *Three Pals* (uncredited)
   The Enchanted Hill (uncredited)
   The Johnstown Flood (uncredited)
   A Six Shootin' Romance (uncredited)
   Watch Your Wife (uncredited)
   Thundering Speed (uncredited)
   Lightnin' Wins
   The Winning of Barbara Worth

Lightnin' Flashes (unconfirmed)
Old Ironsides (uncredited)
Bad Man's Bluff (uncredited)
It (uncredited)

1927   *Arizona Bound*
       Children of Divorce
       The Last Outlaw
       Wings
       Nevada

1928   *Half a Bride*
       Beau Sabreur
       Doomsday
       The Legion of the Condemned
       Red Hair
       Lilac Time
       The First Kiss
       The Shopworn Angel

1929   *The Wolf Song*
       Betrayal
       The Virginian

1930   *Seven Days' Leave*
       Only the Brave
       Paramount on Parade
       The Texan
       A Man from Wyoming
       Galas de la Paramount
       The Spoilers
       Morocco

1931   *Fighting Caravans*
        The Slippery Pearls
        City Streets
        I Take This Woman
        His Woman

1932   *Devil and the Deep*
        If I Had a Million
        A Farewell to Arms

1933   *Today We Live*
        One Sunday Afternoon
        Alice in Wonderland
        Design for Living

1934   *Operator 13*
        Now and Forever

1935   *The Lives of a Bengal Lancer*
        The Wedding Night
        Peter Ibbetson

1936   *Desire*
        Mr. Deeds Goes to Town (Oscar nomination for
            Best Actor in a Leading Role)
        Hollywood Boulevard
        The General Died at Dawn
        The Plainsman

1937   *Lest We Forget*
        Souls at Sea

1938   *Bluebeard's Eighth Wife*
        The Adventures of Marco Polo
        The Cowboy and the Lady

1939 *Beau Geste*
      The Real Glory
1940 *The Westerner*
      North West Mounted Police
1941 *Meet John Doe*
      Sergeant York (Oscar win for Best Actor in a
          Leading Role)
      Ball of Fire
1942 *The Pride of the Yankees* (Oscar nomination for
          Best Actor in a Leading Role)
1943 *For Whom the Bell Tolls* (Oscar nomination for
          Best Actor in a Leading Role)
1944 *The Story of Dr. Wassell*
      Casanova Brown
1945 *Along Came Jones*
      Saratoga Trunk
1946 *Cloak and Dagger*
1947 *Unconquered*
1948 *Good Sam*
1949 *Snow Carnival* (voice: Narrator)
      The Fountainhead
      It's a Great Feeling
      Task Force
1950 *Bright Leaf*
      Dallas
1951 *You're in the Navy Now*
      It's a Big Country
      Distant Drums

1952   *High Noon* (Oscar win for Best Actor in a
          Leading Role)
        Springfield Rifle

1953   *Return to Paradise*
        Blowing Wild

1954   *Garden of Evil*
        Vera Cruz

1955   *The Court-Martial of Billy Mitchell*

1956   *Friendly Persuasion*

1957   *Love in the Afternoon*

1958   *Ten North Frederick*
        Man of the West

1959   *The Hanging Tree*
        Alias Jesse James (uncredited)
        They Came to Cordura
        The Wreck of the Mary Deare

1961   *The Naked Edge*

Picture Credits